Martial **Mechanics**

Also by Phillip Starr

*The Making of a Butterfly: Traditional Chinese Martial Arts
as Taught by W. C. Chen*

Martial
Mechanics

Maximum Results with Minimum Effort in the Practice of the Martial Arts

Phillip Starr

BLUE SNAKE BOOKS
Berkeley, California

Published by Blue Snake Books

Blue Snake Books' publications are distributed by
North Atlantic Books
P.O. Box 12327
Berkeley, California 94712

Cover photo by Alanda Foster
Cover and book design by Brad Greene
Photographs by Alanda Foster

Printed in the United States of America

Blue Snake Books publications are available through most bookstores. For further information, call 800-733-3000 or visit our Web sites at www.northatlanticbooks.com and www.bluesnakebooks.com.

Martial Mechanics: Maximum Results with Minimum Effort in the Practice of Martial Arts is sponsored by the Society for the Study of Native Arts and Sciences, a nonprofit educational corporation whose goals are to develop an educational and cross-cultural perspective linking various scientific, social, and artistic fields; to nurture a holistic view of arts, sciences, humanities, and healing; and to publish and distribute literature on the relationship of mind, body, and nature.

PLEASE NOTE: The creators and publishers of this book are not and will not be responsible, in any way whatsoever, for any improper use made by anyone of the information contained in this book. All use of the aforementioned information must be made in accordance with what is permitted by law, and any damage liable to be caused as a result thereof will be the exclusive responsibility of the user. In addition, he or she must adhere strictly to the safety rules contained in the book, both in training and in actual implementation of the information presented herein. This book is intended for use in conjunction with ongoing lessons and personal training with an authorized expert. It is not a substitute for formal training. It is the sole responsibility of every person planning to train in the techniques described in this book to consult a licensed physician in order to obtain complete medical information on his or her personal ability and limitations. The instructions and advice printed in this book are not in any way intended as a substitute for medical, mental, or emotional counseling with a licensed physician or healthcare provider.

Library of Congress Cataloging-in-Publication Data

Starr, Phillip.
  Martial mechanics : maximum results with minimum effort in the practice of martial arts / by Phillip Starr.
       p. cm.
    Summary: "Martial Mechanics describes the principles upon which traditional martial arts techniques are based, explaining how laws of physics and principles of Kinesiology affect techniques and how one can utilize these laws to make techniques faster, more powerful, and more effective in combat"—Provided by publisher.
    Includes bibliographical references.
    ISBN 978-1-58394-211-6 (trade paper)
    1. Martial arts. 2. Martial arts—Study and teaching. I. Title.
    GV1101.S73 2008
    796.81—dc22
                                                                                      CIP

2 3 4 5 6 7 8 9 SHERIDAN 14 13 12 11 10 09 08

Dedication

To my teacher, Master W. C. Chen,
and his devoted wife, Mei.
I promised that your legacy would continue.
And I meant it.

Contents

Acknowledgments

I owe a debt of thanks to my wonderful students, Sifu Vince Hardy (Chief Instructor, Yiliquan Martial Arts Association), Jeremy Thompson, Susan Brown, and Matt Schumacher, who gave so freely of their time in posing as models.

I'd also like to acknowledge the hard work and dedication of my adopted daughter and former student, Ms. Alanda Foster (Women's Midwest Middleweight Kickboxing Champion, retired undefeated), who not only served as a model but also donated her time and expertise as a photographer.

And I owe special thanks to three extraordinary ladies: Ms. Anastasia McGhee, Ms. Yvonne Cárdenas, and Ms. Allegra Harris of North Atlantic/Frog Ltd./Blue Snake Books. Their extraordinary patience and professional (but ever so gentle) guidance made this book possible.

Foreword

Before you read any farther I must warn you that there are no "silver bullets" in this book—no secret techniques that will turn you into an invincible martial arts hero who stands for truth, justice, and mom's rice pudding. However, if you're sincerely interested in learning the principles upon which traditional martial arts are based and how you can utilize these principles to make your own techniques faster, stronger, and more effective, the information you seek is in here. In any case, most bookstores won't give you a refund on this book, so if you've already paid for it you're stuck with it. You might as well read it and see if there's something worth your while between its covers.

And there is. Lots.

I've tried to present the material in a manner that's simple and easy to understand, but also playful. I must confess that there's a fair dose of irreverence tossed into the mix, too. I don't know about you, but I'm tired of martial arts books that sound so … well, *sterile*. So, don't be offended if I heckle you now and then. It's nothing personal. I just wanted this text to have some life and character to it—a martial arts book that's fun to read as well as educational.

Why?

Hearken back to your school days—the ones you didn't skip. From which teachers did you learn most readily? I'm willing to bet that the instructors you recall most vividly are the ones who made you laugh while you learned. It's easier to learn when you're smiling.

And learning is what counts.

Introduction

I've been involved in the martial arts for most of my life. I began my martial arts career in 1956 as the youngest student in a small judo club on a military base in the Panama Canal Zone. Since then, I have trained in traditional *baixingquan* (a form of northern *Shao-lin kung-fu*), *taijiquan*, *xingyiquan*, *baguazhang*, the karate styles of *Kyokushin* and *Shito-ryu*, and the Pekiti-Tersia style of Filipino *arnis*.

In the late 1950s and early '60s the Asian martial arts were still very new to the Occident. Oriental instructors who hoped to spread the gospel of their respective disciplines while simultaneously preserving their fundamental principles and traditions provided most of the available instruction. For the most part they were successful, but with the passage of time, things changed dramatically.

Having been involved in the martial arts for more than fifty years, I can bear witness to the various transformations that martial arts techniques have undergone in the last few decades. The development and subsequent popularity of tournaments resulted in many martial disciplines becoming "sportified." Myriad martial arts enthusiasts became enthralled with the idea of competition—of becoming famous champions and winning huge trophies. And various instructors began emphasizing the scoring of points above and beyond the practice of traditional technique. Consequently, many of the original principles upon which martial arts techniques are based were ignored and, in some cases, forgotten altogether.

I watched as traditional techniques were modified to accommodate their use in the tournament arena, particularly after the wearing of foam-padded gloves and footgear became widespread. It was inevitable that full-contact karate (which was neither full-contact, nor was it really karate) would come along. Just as the original bare-knuckled punching techniques of Western boxing were eventually altered to accommodate the use of the legally mandated boxing glove, continued use of hand and foot pads in karate competitions ultimately resulted in further modifications (and, in my view, deterioration) of traditional punching, striking, and kicking techniques.

The fated decline of full-contact karate led to the development of new forms of competition—events that currently receive billing as "martial arts" but which, in fact, more closely resemble professional wrestling on amphetamines. Many contemporary martial arts instructors and students have tired of the charade. They are fed up with seeing gymnasts and semi-professional wrestlers labeled as martial artists. They want to return to their roots. They want to return to the practice of *real* martial arts and to the kind of technique that made these arts and their devotees the stuff of legend. Unfortunately, they often lack a firm understanding of the principles upon which these techniques are based. It is for these people that I have written this book.

Chapter 1

The Way We Were

Differences

There was a time when many practitioners of the martial arts earned their livelihoods by working as professional soldiers, bodyguards, convoy escorts, or policemen. Such occupations were fraught with danger and only a few survived long enough to retire. These people were extremely serious and very diligent in their practice of martial arts because they knew that their lives would frequently depend upon their fighting prowess. Close-quarters combat was studied in minute detail as each warrior sought that special "extra edge" that might very well mean the difference between life and death.

Many fighters spent most of their lives developing and refining their techniques, and those that worked well are still with us today, preserved within certain traditional martial arts systems. As for those that didn't ... well, they were buried along with their creators who perished in battle, believing that their flawed techniques or tactics were the greatest thing since polished rice.

In those days it was pretty easy to determine whether your technique was truly effective. If it wasn't, you died.

Politics and the advent of firearms put an end to the era of the sword-toting, iron-fisted warriors, and many of these battle-tested veterans turned to competition as a means of refining their techniques and enhancing their fighting abilities. Because many participants were seriously injured or even killed in these brutal contests, viable rules had to be established. Thus, many of the techniques that had once been highly effective in battle were either diluted or banned from the competition arena altogether.

Nowadays, scores of martial arts enthusiasts train primarily for competition rather than for actual life-and-death conflicts. That's fine, so long as they understand that there's a world of difference between competition and combat. In real self-defense there's no second-place winner. There are no trophies, no safety pads, no referees, and *no rules*. What works in the tournament arena won't necessarily work on the street, and what works on the street is often prohibited in competition.

Let me take a moment here to make a few new friends by stating that, in my opinion, the use of the padded glove is one of the worst calamities ever to befall the martial arts. Why do I say that? Well, let's begin by taking a stroll down History Lane and recall the bare-knuckle boxers of the nineteenth and early twentieth centuries.

The boxers of those bygone days frequently employed linear punches because these direct thrusts are fast and difficult to block. Many an aspiring champion was knocked senseless as a result of being on the receiving end of such direct techniques and more than a few lost their lives in these old "rock 'em, sock 'em" bouts. Then, in the late 1860s the Marquis of Queensbury rules were introduced and competitors were subsequently required to wear padded gloves. The authorities emphasized that the use of these gloves would curtail the number and severity of the injuries that had become all too common in the sport. However, the combatants weren't particularly interested in the well-being of their adversaries and they immediately commenced to ascertain just how they could best employ this new device to kayo their opponents.

They discovered pretty quickly that the glove actually *altered the striking surface of the fist*. A straight punch was much less effective with the hand encased in an oversized, padded mitten because the force of the blow was decentralized. This led to an increased reliance on circular, hooking punches that generate considerable power along the outer corners of the gloves due to centrifugal force (Figure 1-1).

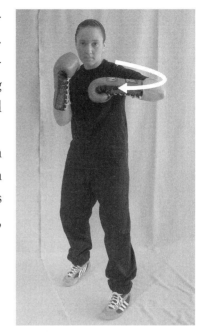

This type of arcing punch works fine so long as a padded glove is worn. But when it is applied with a bare fist, the result is often the classical "boxer's break," wherein the fifth, and sometimes the fourth, metacarpals are fractured.

Additionally, the gloves could be placed against the sides of the head to form a crude shield that offered protection against incoming blows. This tactic works well in the ring but trying to form a shield with your bare fists presents an obvious problem (Figures 1-2 and 1-3).

Figure 1-1

Figure 1-2

Figure 1-3

The art of boxing was gradually reconstructed around the use of the glove, and the "manly art of self-defense" was changed forever. When padded gloves and footgear were first introduced to the martial arts tournament scene, promoters touted them as devices that would minimize the chances of injury.

Yeah, you bet. Hadn't someone made that same statement before? It didn't take long for competitors to figure out that the effectiveness of many traditional techniques was considerably reduced when the hands and feet were encased in thick, foam pads and, as had happened in the sport of boxing some one hundred years earlier, wide hooking punches began to appear. Even some of the basic kicking techniques were modified to accommodate the use of the padded footgear. Within a decade many karate competitors had reconfigured their techniques to accommodate the gloves and footgear. Traditional techniques began to disappear altogether.

What's Real and What Isn't

There are those who say that the traditional martial arts are no longer suitable for self-defense in our modern world. They claim that these antiquated disciplines require too much training and that their adherence to traditional technique stifles individual creativity. People who lack a true, in-depth understanding of the authentic martial arts or who have never been in a real, old-fashioned, full-tilt boogie fight to the finish (or both) often make such imbecilic statements.

Bear in mind that the original martial arts systems were devised by warriors who had actually engaged in genuine life-and-death conflicts ... and survived. They tended to be more than a little persnickety about training with the techniques they'd contrived because they understood the true nature of combat. The object wasn't simply to land a hit, score a point, or pin the opponent to the ground until he cried "uncle!" The object was to dispatch (which is a politically correct way of saying kill) the enemy as quickly as possible. Period. Lengthy Hollywood-style fights, especially the type that include spinning kicks to the head and flying somersaults, never happened.

Let's take a look at some hard facts about self-defense in the real world:

- Rarely will you have the opportunity to assume some kind of formal "on-guard" posture. The "bushwhack" is usually the sleaze-bag's favorite tactic and he will attack when he thinks you're the most physically and/or mentally vulnerable. He loves surprises. Ever hear of a sucker punch?

- Street fighters are tough. If they weren't, they wouldn't last long on the streets. If you hit one of these guys, you'd better hurt him. A *lot*. Once he's hurt, close in and finish the fight. Don't opt for simply landing a hit. That may just serve to whet his appetite for more.

- Lone wolves usually don't live too long. That's why wolves hunt in packs. Scumbags exhibit this same kind of behavior. Rarely will you be faced with a single assailant. It may appear that your opponent is flying solo, but you must never assume that he is. Remember that to *assume* makes an *ass* out of *u* and *me*. Just because you don't *see* the other members of the pack doesn't mean they're not there. They may very well be hiding in the wings, waiting for the chance to jump in and finish you off.

- As a continuation of the previous statement, do not attempt to wrestle your foe to the ground. His buddies probably won't stand around and admire your cute little *tush* while you roll around on the asphalt. Nay, they will step in and bring the conflict to a quick halt by turning you into a wet spot.

- And anyway, just what do you plan to do with the aforementioned bad guy if you *do* pin him to the ground? You can't just lie there and embrace this nasty character all night. If he tells you that he'll be a nice guy and promises not to hit you again, are you going to believe him? If you do, we need to talk.

- In most altercations the bad guy will be armed. His weapon of choice could be anything from a blade to a length of cable or a firearm. He may or may not choose to use it, but rest assured that he's got some kind of trump card concealed on his person and you'd better be prepared to deal with it.

- Even if you can't see him, it is certain that Mr. Murphy (of "Murphy's Law" fame) will be along for the ride. He's best known for advancing his famous principle that says, "If anything can possibly go wrong, it will … and always at the worst possible moment." However, Mr. Murphy also authored a martial art book entitled *When Bad Things Happen to Good Techniques*. You won't find it in any bookstores but Murphy-san will be more than happy to quote some passages from it when you least need to hear them.

The point is that you simply don't have time for a long, drawn-out bout of fisticuffs. You have to be able to hit hard and fast with maximum destructive power. Understanding how certain scientific principles can be applied to your technique will enable you to achieve this goal. Got it? Good. Now, let's get to work.

Chapter 2

Principles of Power

Basic Principles of Force

When I first began training in the martial arts in the late 1950s, many people believed that high-level martial arts "experts" possessed some kind of supernormal power that enabled them to strike with such terrible speed and force that they could easily kill a man with a single blow. My classmates and I did our best to imitate our teachers, but the force we generated was slow, heavy, and awkward.

My kung-fu teacher, the late W. C. Chen, conducted classes in the basement of his home in McLean, Virginia. Like most Chinese, he wasn't very large—probably 125 pounds soaking wet and after a hefty meal—but he had a punch like the hammer of Thor.

On a hot and humid summer afternoon my classmates and I practiced our basic punching techniques for what seemed like a couple of hours. In reality it was probably only ten minutes but we were all soaked with sweat and sucking air when Chen grimaced, stood up, and told us to stop.

"Do not punch with your fist," Chen told us as he held his fist up for all to see. *Okay ... just what do I punch with?*

"Hit with the whole body," he said, as he swept his hands down the sides of his torso.

I envisioned hurling myself into the enemy. *Nah, that can't be right. You punch with your fist! How on earth can I punch with my body?*

Before I embarrassed myself by asking the obvious and revealing my ignorance, Chen proceeded to demonstrate what he meant. He drove forward and fired off one punch after another. I knew that if he ever hit me with one of those thrusts it'd probably cut me in half.

"Punch with the power of the whole body, not just the fist!" Chen growled. "Power comes up from the feet—not from your arm. Punch very fast! Whole body moves into the punch, you see?"

It made sense and sounded easy enough to do, but Chen made it clear that I still needed a lot more practice.

"Where did you learn to punch like that?" he asked.

I had studied a form of karate prior to training with Chen and I told him that that was where I had learned my basic punching technique. I was doing it exactly as my previous instructor had taught me.

Chen shook his head. "I don't care where you learned it! It is *wrong*!" After class I sat down with my teacher and asked him why the various forms of kung-fu, karate, and other martial arts all seem to punch differently.

"A real punch is more than just slapping somebody with your fist," he said. "If you only want to make a hit, it's easy. Anyone can do that. But if you want to develop the power to knock a man down with one punch, you must study the principles involved. It doesn't matter whether you train in karate, Shao-lin, xingyiquan [a form of internal kung-fu], or anything else. If you want real power, you must use the right principles."

And so it was that I realized that, regardless of which martial art we practice, we're all governed by the same unalterable laws of physics and kinesiology, and in order to maximize the effectiveness of our techniques, we must learn how to apply these principles to our best advantage. Understanding how these laws affect our movements and techniques enables us to learn how to fully utilize the strength of the whole body. Correct movement also facilitates the emission of intrinsic energy (known as *qi* in Chinese and *ki* in Japanese).

Conversely, failure to adhere to these laws of (human) motion will result in a loss of power and stability because we restrict ourselves to using the isolated strength of the individual limbs. It also reduces our ability to emit intrinsic energy because qi is expressed through our physical bodies only when the qi channels are open and unrestricted by "kinks" that result from incorrect postures or movements.

Physics and the Martial Arts

Yeah, I saw the look on your face as you read the first word of the subheading, "Physics." And you're wondering just what physics has to do with martial arts.

Everything.

If you want to strike with greater force, you have to understand the physical principles involved and how to use them. So, don't just leaf through this section like you used to do in your science class. Sit down and study this stuff. It's going to make a real difference in your technique.

Measuring Force

F = ma. That is, force (F) equals mass (m) multiplied by the acceleration (a) of that mass. The more you have of both, the more force you will generate. That's pretty easy to understand, isn't it? But we need to go one step farther. We need to examine these two components individually and how the equation F = ma is applied to punching someone in the mouth.

First, let's establish a clear definition of what constitutes *mass*. As far as we're concerned, your mass is equal to your body weight. However, you cannot strike your opponent with the power of your *entire* mass unless you're performing a flying tackle or being used as a human battering ram. A flying tackle may work well in a football game but it's a pretty risky maneuver to attempt when you're engaged in a *mano y mano* confrontation.

In combat it's crucial that you maintain complete control of your balance at all times. In order to do this you can utilize only about 50 to 60 percent of your mass in the performance of any given technique. If you attempt to use any more than that you'll hyperextend your technique and lose your balance. So, the force you generate is equal to *the mass that's involved in the execution of the technique*, multiplied by its acceleration.

Yeah, I can hear you griping, "I can use only half my mass? Why half? I want to use *all* my mass and punch like a freight train!"

Well, if you're absolutely determined to use all of your mass, join the circus and become a human cannonball. However, if you want to improve your martial arts technique, quit interrupting me and listen up.

The second half of the equation involves acceleration. Although many martial arts zealots like to think that their punches and kicks travel at something approaching Mach 2, the truth is often rather disheartening. Many years ago, a prominent Japanese karate organization conducted experiments to determine the speed of various techniques performed by students of different grades. The punch of a beginning student was found to be around 16 mph, which is actually faster than you might think. Most physicists measure velocity and acceleration in terms of meters per second (m/s). So, 16 mph is equal to about 8 m/s. It may not *sound* fast but, trust me, if you get hit with a punch traveling at that pace, it'll rock your world! Lower-grade black belts could punch at speeds up to 30 mph, which is equal to about 15 m/s. It's not exactly warp speed but it's plenty fast. Think about a fist that's only 4 feet away from you blazing into your muzzle at that velocity! Now let's take a look at the amount of force you can generate when you launch your best punch. Let's say that you weigh 180 pounds and that you can punch at a maximum velocity of 20 mph. We begin by halving the mass (180 pounds), because you can only employ about half of it in the performance of your technique, right? This means that your punch will make use of 90 pounds of your mass. So, the formula would read F = 90 lbs multiplied by 9 m/s (okay, go ahead and use 20 mph). Now, do the math.

The amount of force you'll calculate is enormously powerful! It's enough to drop a horse! But before you go into a wild frenzy and start tearing through the phone book looking for the nearest stables, you need to realize that due to certain variables, you're going to lose much of that power.

Sorry. You should've known that it was too good to be true, but look on the bright side: Even if you lose up to half of that power you'll retain more than enough to drop even the largest opponent. Moreover, all of that force is concentrated onto the striking surface of your technique, which is one of the things that make martial arts techniques so lethal.

Concentrated Striking Force

The force you generate with your technique has to be divided by the size of the striking surface of your bodily weapon. The striking surface of most hand weapons is about a square inch or perhaps a little more. So, if you're punching with the first two knuckles of your fist (which is about a square inch), the force generated will be figured in pounds per square inch. Other striking surfaces, like those of the feet, are considerably larger.

Imagine what would happen if you were lying on your back with a one-inch peg on your chest and your training partner dropped a hundred-pound weight on it! It'd probably leave a real nasty mark (on your liver) and that's only 100 pounds per square inch (psi). I'll wager that the amount of force you figured you could muster was a good deal more than that!

Of course, the real trick is to execute and apply your technique as perfectly as possible, thereby minimizing the amount of power you'll inevitably lose. This involves a lot more than you might think. Just because a technique *looks* correct doesn't mean that it *is* correct. What happens *inside* is at least as important as what happens *outside*. You don't want your technique to become like a sprinkled doughnut with lots of glitz on the outside but nothing on the inside where it really matters.

Is Bigger Better?

If two fighters punch or kick at the same velocity, the larger fighter will usually strike with greater force simply because he can bring more mass into play than the lighter combatant. In reality, however, a number of factors have to be considered:

- No two fighters will ever really strike at exactly the same velocity. One will always be faster than the other.
- Although the larger fighter has more mass at his disposal, he may not utilize it effectively if his technique or body movement is flawed. In fact, it's entirely possible that he'll strike with less mass than the smaller fighter. Of course, the same thing may be true of the smaller fighter.
- A smaller fighter can maximize the effects of his blows by striking into his opponent's vital points.
- If you bother to delve further into this book, you'll discover how and why the smaller fighter can dramatically increase his striking power by boosting the velocity of his techniques (see Chapter 4).

- If the smaller fighter reads Chapter 16, he'll learn how he can use the larger fighter's strength against him!

A Ton of Power

Correct martial arts technique is capable of generating enormous power. One of the strongest punches ever measured was executed by a small, 110-pound Okinawan karate practitioner. He was able to generate approximately *2,000 pounds of force* with his thrust! Compare this to the legendary Muhammad Ali's punch, which produced about 1,000 pounds of force!

Chapter 3

The Big Bang

Making an Impact

The *real* martial arts are much more than simply hauling off and whacking your opponent as hard as you can. Any chump can do that. Authentic martial arts teach you how to mete out *different types of impact*. The type of impact you produce depends upon what technique and body movements you use, the surface you intend to strike, and the effect(s) you intend to visit upon that surface and the tissues that lie beneath it.

This is important stuff, so don't skip it. It's one of the key differences between martial arts and brawling.

Target Surfaces

When you punch a human body, do you punch it in the same way as you do a heavy bag? Have you ever considered that humans aren't structured at all like heavy, cotton-filled canvas or vinyl bags? Well, since you're more likely to have to defend yourself against a human being than a contentious heavy bag, it's a good idea to acquire a basic understanding of just what it is that you're going to be hitting. There are three basic types of surfaces on the human body:

- *Soft surfaces* are areas that are not protected by bones. They are covered with layers of muscle and fat that help to protect the viscera and other vital tissues lying beneath them. The abdominal area is the best example of a soft surface.

The force of your blows must be capable of penetrating through these protective tissues to affect the vital targets that lie beneath them. This isn't too difficult if you're striking into thinly shielded areas such as the sides of the neck or throat. However, when you strike into the abdominal area your technique must generate considerable shock in order to damage the viscera that lie beneath the thicker and stronger layers of muscle and fat.

- *Hard surfaces* are areas where flesh and thin layers of muscle are stretched tight over bony structures. These include the head and face, wrists, toes, and fingers.

  Damaging these surfaces and/or the vital tissues located beneath them is not particularly difficult because they aren't well protected by thick layers of muscle.

- *Hard-soft surfaces* are areas where some substantial amount of muscle and fatty tissue cover a bony structure. The thighs, calves, upper arms, and forearms are good examples.

Types of Impact

It may surprise you to know that a punch, a backfist strike, an elbow smash, and a front kick do not all necessarily generate the same kind of impact. "So what?" you ask. "As long as I hit my opponent, what difference does it make?"

A big difference.

Every striking technique is specifically designed to produce a particular type of impact. If you're lumping all of your techniques into a single impact category with the object being simply to hit the enemy as hard as you can, you're using what I call the "tastes like chicken" approach. And that isn't martial arts. It's just a spiffed-up donnybrook.

There are four basic categories of impact. These include *focused impact, piercing impact, snap-back impact,* and *smashing impact.* Let's briefly examine each one.

Focused Impact

To understand how this kind of impact works, let's begin by having you hearken back to the days when you were actually awake in your science class. ... Now, complete this sentence:

The human body is approximately 60 percent _____.

No, the answer is not beer! But if you guessed that the answer is water, you're absolutely right! Heavy bags have minimal water content but humans are mostly water. They're like thick-skinned balloons filled with H_2O (and sometimes beer). So, in order to inflict maximum damage on a human target, you must learn how to generate *hydrostatic shock.* And that's just what *focused impact* does. When contact is made with the target, the technique is brought to a sudden stop. It doesn't penetrate deeply nor does it snap back quickly. The power of the blow is focused through, rather than on, a particular point. The shocking force of this kind of blow will penetrate deeply into the interior of the opponent, causing severe internal damage.

An example of this form of impact is shown in Figure 3-1, which illustrates a fist striking a water-filled balloon. The force of the blow travels *through* the target and causes the far side of the balloon to expand.

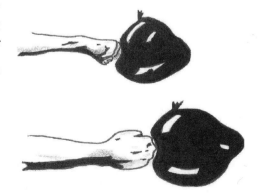

Figure 3-1

Most punching and striking techniques, as well as kicking techniques that utilize a knee snap, fall into the focused-impact category. This type of blow can be applied to virtually any target surface (see Figures 3-2 to 3-5).

Figure 3-2

Figure 3-3

Figure 3-4

Figure 3-5

Piercing Impact

Piercing impact techniques are used to penetrate into the target surface. They are very few in number and consist mainly of techniques that utilize the fingertips or second knuckles to thrust into the softer surfaces of the body. Although they generate a *secondary reaction force* (see Chapter 5), the shock that they induce is considerably different from the kind of shock engendered by focused-impact techniques. Figure 3-6 illustrates how this form of shock operates. You'll notice that the far side of the balloon doesn't necessarily bulge out very far. Most of the shock is focused on the actual site of penetration.

Figure 3-6

To be able to use piercing-impact techniques skillfully usually requires special (and often painful) training exercises that are intended to strengthen and toughen the fingers and knuckles. Certain types of kicks may also be employed to penetrate the surface of the target (see Figures 3-7 to 3-9).

Figure 3-7   **Figure 3-8**   **Figure 3-9**

It should be noted that *literal* penetration is not the intention of these techniques. Imagine thrusting the end of a broomstick into your assailant's belly or throat. A strong thrust can easily inflict severe internal damage without actually penetrating the flesh. And anyway, piercing human flesh with the fingertips is very nearly impossible. Even so, if I had a nickel for every blowhard who claimed that he or his uncle could thrust his fingertips into an assailant's chest cavity and rip out his heart, I'd have retired a long time ago. If you know somebody who makes this kind of claim, you might suggest that he open a drive-through surgical service.

Snap-Back Impact

Snap-back impact is generated by techniques such as the backfist strikes. Because these techniques have very little penetration, they are best employed against bony surfaces such as the head and face (Figures 3-10 and 3-11).

Figure 3-10

Figure 3-11

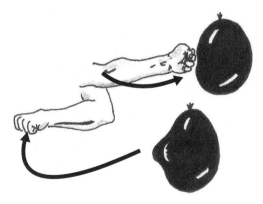

Figure 3-12

Although they're in contact with the hard surface of the target for only a fraction of a second, these whip-like techniques create a very sharp and focused form of shock. In fact, when properly applied, they can cause bone to shatter! This is due to the large amount of force generated due to *impulse* (see Chapter 6). Figure 3-12 shows how this form of shock would affect our balloon.

Smashing Impact

Smashing impact is produced by stamping kicks, free-swinging circular kicks, flying kicks, boxing-style punches, kicks made with the knees, and forearm smashes. These types of blows are usually directed at hard or hard-soft surfaces where bone can be shattered. They don't generate shock because their power is not sharply focused and doesn't necessarily bore deeply into the target.

These techniques rely entirely on momentum and are akin to hitting the enemy with an axe handle. The objective is simply to crush the target on impact (Figures 3-13 to 3-15).

Figure 3-13

Figure 3-14

Figure 3-15

The Chinese *neijia* (forms of internal martial arts) teach a few additional forms of impact, but they are beyond the scope of this basic text. Maybe if enough people buy this book, I'll write a sequel and discuss these methods.

Chapter 4

The Need for Speed

The Secret of Kinetic Energy

Kinetic energy is the energy of motion. It's determined by multiplying half of the mass (which is used in the execution of the technique) by the square of its velocity ($KE = 1/2m \times v^2$). This means that the *faster* you strike, the *harder* you strike.

You already know that momentum is directly proportional to the mass multiplied by its acceleration to a final velocity at impact, right? Well, kinetic energy is directly proportional to the *square of the velocity!* If you want to hit with greater destructive power, don't worry about pumping huge amounts of iron or slugging down those ultra-yummy protein shakes every day to increase your mass. Instead, train to increase the velocity of your techniques! Just think; if you can double the speed of your punch or kick, the kinetic energy that you generate isn't merely doubled; it's increased by a factor of four. It quadruples!

Terminal Velocity

What can you do to increase the velocity of your techniques? The answer is that you must first learn how to execute your techniques correctly. Correct techniques have built-in mechanisms, which are intended to maximize acceleration and velocity. If your punch or kick is weak, it may be that it lacks adequate acceleration due to improper body movement or breathing.

For instance, when you execute a punch, the fist should screw over at the instant just before impact (Figures 4-1 to 4-3).

Figure 4-1   **Figure 4-2**   **Figure 4-3**

You say that you already knew that? Fine, but do you know *why* it's important? The screwing of the fist, whether it is a half-twist or only a quarter-twist, actually has two primary functions:

- To cause the striking force to spiral like a bullet as it speeds toward its target. This spiraling action allows the energy of the blow to penetrate more deeply into the target than would otherwise be possible.

- To produce a dramatic *acceleration* of the technique just prior to impact. Once the screwing movement has been completed, a significant *deceleration* occurs. Novices often fail to understand the importance of this seemingly inconsequential movement. They screw the fist over prematurely, shortly after the punch has been initiated. This means that the thrust is decelerating and losing power when it hits the target.

Most striking and thrusting techniques utilize some kind of screwing or snapping movement in the wrist just prior to contact with the opponent. Figures 4-4 to 4-7 show how it is used in the execution of basic sword-hand strikes.

Figure 4-4

Figure 4-5

Figure 4-6

Figure 4-7

Many contemporary martial arts practitioners are unaware that the front snap kick and side thrust kick also employ this principle. A slight downward snap of the ankle provides a sudden *increase in acceleration* just before the foot strikes the target. These two kicks are chambered in exactly the same position. In the case of the front snap kick, the ankle snaps forward and down just before impact. When you perform a side thrust kick, the ankle snaps down so that contact is made with the outer edge of the heel (Figures 4-8 to 4-10).

Figure 4-8

Figure 4-9

Figure 4-10

Longer Is Better

If I throw a rock at you from a distance of only 2 feet it probably won't do much damage, right? But if I back up several yards and hurl the same rock it will strike you with considerably more force. The reason is:

The greater the distance over which a force accelerates, the more power it accumulates.

Why?

Because as it accelerates, it gains more velocity and, hence, momentum! However, the force must constantly accelerate in order to gather power. Once it begins to decelerate it loses power. Therefore, it behooves you to figure out how to maximize the distance that your technique accelerates. The greater that distance, the harder you'll hit.

Most novices punch only with the movement of the arm. The distance the force travels is only an arm's length (Figure 4-11).

Once the neophyte learns to utilize the movement of his waist, the distance doubles (Figure 4-12).

After some considerable practice the student learns to bring the force of his blow up from the sole of his driving foot. This triples the distance over which the force of his technique accelerates, enabling him to strike with much greater force (Figure 4-13).

Can this distance be increased any more? You bet it can!

Figure 4-11

Figure 4-12

Figure 4-13

Coiling Power

Practitioners of the Chinese internal martial arts are able to markedly increase the distance over which the force and energy of their techniques travel, by utilizing a special type of technique that causes the force to spiral upward from the sole of the driving foot. Each internal system calls it by a different name but the best known is *chan-si jin*, which is a term used by taijiquan stylists. It sounds rather exotic but the underlying theory behind it isn't particularly difficult to understand. Let's start with a basic analogy.

If you want to boost the reception of the radio in your automobile, you can fasten a short cylindrical coil (which consists of several yards of additional antenna) to the original antenna. This will increase the efficiency of your radio several times. The same principle is used in the generation of chan-si jin. The rear foot is "screwed" down into the ground at the very beginning of the movement. The power is made to spiral up the leg, around the waist, up and over the back and shoulder, down the arm, and out to the striking surface of the hand where it is finally released. This will dramatically increase the distance over which the force accelerates, adding tremendous impetus to the blow (see Figure 4-14).

Chan-si jin is translated as "silk reeling power" because of its similarity to pulling a strand of silk from the cocoon of the silkworm. As the strand is pulled, the cocoon rotates. If you stop pulling momentarily and then attempt to begin pulling again, the silk strand will break.

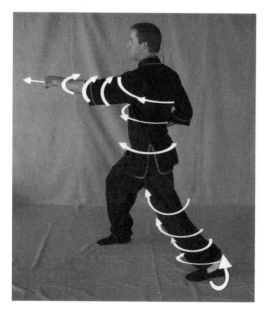

Figure 4-14

Just as the delicate silk fiber must be drawn evenly and smoothly, so the spiraling movement of power in your body must travel without slowing down or stopping momentarily at any given point. Such interference severs the smooth transmission of power and much of it will be lost. If you want to learn more about this special method of issuing power, you must seek out a qualified instructor of the Chinese internal martial arts.

Common Errors

Training to increase the speed and acceleration of your techniques takes time. If you hurry, the odds are that you'll injure yourself, probably by hyperextending an elbow or knee. Study this list of common errors.

- *When executing a given technique, use no more muscular tension than is absolutely necessary.* Tensed muscles don't move very quickly. When you punch, don't clench your fist tightly. Squeezing the fist causes excessive tension in the wrist and forearm.
- *If you're unstable your technique cannot accelerate properly.* Make sure you're in a solid, stable position when you perform your technique.
- *Don't slam the elbow or knee into a straightened, locked position.* For one thing, this is an excellent way to hyperextend the joint and possibly damage it.

  Also, when the returning *reaction force* passes through a locked joint, it may cause damage. Go to Chapter 5 and review the first item in the Common Errors section. Your bodily weapon must be able to withstand the full force of your own blow! Once the force of your blow has been initially transmitted into your opponent and travels down to the sole of his rear foot (initial impact), it will "bounce" back to the point of impact. It then returns through your striking limb and back down to your rear foot (reaction force; see Chapter 5). Believe me, you don't want that kind of power traveling through a locked joint!

If you're delivering a punch or a strike, the elbow should be very slightly flexed at the instant of impact. The knee should also be slightly flexed when you strike the opponent with a kicking technique.

- *Correct breathing is essential to maximizing velocity.* If you want to move quickly you must exhale very quickly. If your exhalation is too slow, the speed of your movements will be proportionately affected (see Chapter 9).

Chapter 5

That's Shocking!

Brute Force and Shock

Most of the punching, striking, and kicking techniques of the traditional martial arts endeavor to generate *shock* rather than brute force. Unfortunately, many martial arts practitioners don't know the difference between the two. So, pay attention.

If someone throws a 50-pound bag of sand at you, that's a rough illustration of brute force. The force with which the bag lands will be spread out over a fairly large surface. Its power isn't concentrated on any particular point and the likelihood of a serious injury occurring is fairly minimal. Any Midwestern kid who's ever baled hay is living proof of this fact.

However, if someone drops a 50-pound weight onto a 1-inch peg that's set on your chest (50 psi), the force is concentrated onto a very small point. This kind of power is what we call *shock*. It penetrates through the protective outer layers of muscle and bone, and expends most of its energy *inside* the target. This can cause serious internal damage.

Many martial arts devotees are unable to generate real *shock* with their techniques because they don't understand what it is, how it works, or how to generate it. Let's fix that.

Figure 5-1

Action and Reaction

Surely you remember your beloved science teacher mentioning Newton's Third Law of Motion? It's the one that says:

For every action, there is an equal and opposite reaction.

It is crucial that you learn how this law affects your technique and how to use it to your best advantage.

For instance, when you deliver a powerful blow with one hand, the opposite hand is simultaneously pulled back to your hip or chest (Figure 5-1).

This is an example of how Newton's Third Law of Motion is applied to basic technique. The withdrawal of the non-striking hand actually lends additional force to the blow, and the stronger its withdrawal, the stronger the outgoing punch will be.

Some current martial art devotees insist that this statement isn't valid—that it's just an old-fashioned, stylized way of doing things.

I disagree.

Try this simple experiment: Hold one arm out in front of you. Now, throw a punch as powerfully as you can with your other hand but don't move the extended arm (Figures 5-2 and 5-3).

Can't get much power into your punch, huh? That's because it's *natural* to draw back the extended hand. Your body wants to do it, so listen to your body! Draw that hand back forcefully and you'll notice a real increase in the power of your punch.

Figure 5-2

Figure 5-3

Force, Reaction Force, and Shock

This same law of motion also applies whenever one object collides with another—for example, when your bodily weapon makes contact with the opponent. Before we proceed further with this discussion, you need to know which hand or foot you're using to strike and which foot is your driving foot.

"Just what is a *driving foot?*" you ask. The driving foot is the foot that presses against the ground and propels you and/or your technique forward (Figure 5-4).

It's usually, but not always, the rear foot.

Figure 5-4

Figure 5-5

Now that we have that concept in mind, let's take a look at how this whole force and shock thing works, step by step.

1. Your force initially travels from your driving foot to the hand or foot that strikes the opponent. It then enters the opponent's body and travels from the point of impact down to his rearmost foot. This is the *initial impact* (Figure 5-5).

2. The force then *rebounds*. It travels back up through the opponent's body, re-enters your body through your hand or foot (depending upon whether you struck the opponent with a hand blow or a kick), and returns to the point of origin, which is your driving foot. This rebounding force is the *reaction force* that results from the initial impact that you created (Figure 5-6).

If you push against a tree or a wall, you will feel the reaction

Figure 5-6

force travel back through your arm to your shoulder, down your (rear) driving leg, and into your (rear), driving foot. Go ahead, try it. Make sure that you keep your back straight. Don't cheat by leaning into the tree or wall. The harder you push, the more force you'll feel in your back foot. This demonstrates how your initial force returns to its point of origin.

3. If your technique has been performed correctly from a strong, balanced position, the reaction force rebounds! If you're wondering how this is possible, you haven't been paying attention. Go back and re-read Newton's Third Law of Motion, above, and consider this: If your driving foot is pressing firmly against the ground, it creates a force that does what?

   It generates a reaction force!

Figure 5-7

The stronger you press your driving foot into the ground, the stronger your blow will be. It travels up from the sole of your driving foot and enters the target a second time. This is what we call shock, and it penetrates deeply into the target (Figure 5-7). Shock is actually a secondary reaction force.

This secondary reaction force will always follow the line of least resistance, expending most of its energy on the least stable target. If your opponent is off-balance at the instant of impact, he will absorb most of the power of your blow. However, if you're less stable than your opponent, you'll receive the lion's share of the force of your own strike! You must make sure that you're in a firmly rooted posi-

Figure 5-8

Figure 5-9

tion at the moment of impact so that you don't end up eating most of your own force (Figures 5-8 and 5-9).

"So, what's the big deal about hitting someone with this shock?" you ask. "Can't I hurt my opponent if I just use a lot of brute force?"

Sure, you can. But if you use brute force, the amount of damage you'll inflict depends on the strength of your arm relative to the size of your opponent. You're hitting with the isolated power of your arm instead of your whole body and, if your technique is really bad, you may end up pushing your opponent with your fist instead of delivering a sharply focused punch.

If you're an average-sized person of average strength and you use brute force to whack some guy who's built like Mr. Universe, what do you suppose will happen? Well, if he ever finds out about it you could be in real trouble and end up with a nose that looks like a Twinkie that somebody sat on. On the other hand, if you drive in a sharply focused blow, with shock, you could very well turn part of his internal environment into strawberry jam.

A Master's Master

I first met Master Arthur Lee of Honolulu in 1991 at the AAU National Chinese Martial Arts Championships, when we established a wonderful, lifelong friendship. A zealous practitioner of *Fut-Ga* (a southern form of *Shao-lin* boxing, of which he is unquestionably one of the world's leading authorities) and taijiquan, Mr. Lee exemplifies the essence of the word *master*. I am honored to be able to call him one of my dearest and most treasured friends.

Mr. Lee was kind enough to teach a short seminar during halftime at the tournament. One of the techniques he demonstrated was a form of blocking that involved slapping the opponent's attacking arm with his palm. "My teacher could leave a black handprint on your arm by blocking with this technique," he said. "It would leave the impression of his palm and all five fingers."

Naturally, one of the participants asked to see this technique, and as fate would have it, this participant was one of *my* senior students! I held my breath. Mr. Lee accepted the thinly veiled challenge graciously and had the young man fire a strong punch at him. He easily evaded the thrust and lightly slapped his opponent's forearm. My student looked down at his arm. "Huh," he remarked. "That didn't feel like much."

I hid my reddened face in my hands and turned away, knowing full well what would happen next. "That was just a light slap," Mr. Lee explained. "But if you like, I will show you the real thing. Please attack me as powerfully as you can." The young man obliged, launching a full-tilt thrust straight at Mr.

Lee, who calmly sidestepped the blow and smartly slapped the offending limb.

The power of his defensive technique exploded into the youngster's arm and nearly knocked him down. He tenderly rubbed his numbed appendage and within a few seconds a bright red five-fingered handprint appeared on the arm. After about a minute it had turned almost completely black. The young man was so impressed that he ran around the gymnasium, showing his arm to everyone. I'm certain that several competitors thought that his mind had been affected as well as his arm.

It was a fine demonstration of masterful technique. Such skill is rarely seen anymore.

Common Errors

Generating shock isn't nearly as easy as it might seem. There are a lot more ways to perform your technique incorrectly than you might think, and all of them will result in a loss of power. Some of them will prevent you from generating any shock at all. Let's look at a few of the most basic errors.

Figure 5-10

■ *If your bodily weapon or the limb to which it is attached is unable to withstand the force of the blow, your wrist, elbow, or ankle will collapse. If your wrist is bent up or down at the point of impact it will snap backward or crumple downward, often resulting in a painful injury to the joint* (Figure 5-10).

This is why many martial arts schools insist on strengthening the wrists through exercises such as push-ups on the fists or repeatedly striking a punching post.

- *Force tends to travel in a straight line.* If your elbow is well-bent at an outward angle at the moment of impact, just where do you think most of the *reaction force* will go? If you guessed that it will shoot out your elbow and dissipate into space, you're right (Figures 5-11 and 5-12). This kind of blow employs only the strength of the arm rather than the strength of the entire body.

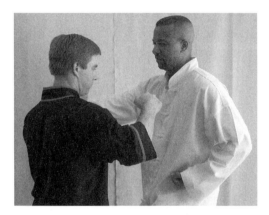

Figure 5-11

Figure 5-12

- *If you're unstable when you strike your target, you will probably provide your foe with a few laughs by knocking yourself off-balance and absorbing the majority of the force that you generate.* You're actually striking yourself! This is dangerous as well as very embarrassing (Figures 5-13 to 5-15).

Figure 5-13

Figure 5-14

Figure 5-15

- *If the heel of your driving foot is raised up, your ankle will absorb most of the reaction force.* The rebounding of the reaction force will not occur and you will be unable to generate shock (Figure 5-16).

Figure 5-16

Striking Through the Target

Martial arts students are often told to "strike through" the surface of the target and to direct their blows at an imaginary point that lies beneath or beyond it. This concept is often introduced to them when they try to break their first board. Beginners are frequently surprised at how this simple mental exercise seems to augment the power and effectiveness of their techniques, but within a few weeks they've usually forgotten about it altogether.

This is unfortunate because it's one of the most important lessons they'll ever learn about the effective application of martial art technique. And why is that?

When you direct a powerful technique into a given target, you tend to tense up certain muscle groups just before impact, depending upon how much resistance you anticipate from the target. For instance, you probably don't tense up at all when you drive a punch into the filled bathtub ... unless there's someone sitting in it. However, when you fire your best punch into a heavy bag or try to shove your fist through several boards, you probably tense up in anticipation of some fairly stout resistance.

And what happens when you tense up just before impact? Your tensed muscles act like brakes and your technique decelerates! This means you're rapidly losing power.

However, when you're aiming at a point *beyond* the exterior of the target, you aren't tensed up at the moment of impact because your mind isn't focused on the surface of the objective in anticipation of resistance. You're relaxed, the brakes aren't engaged, and your technique will strike the target at the highest possible velocity. The *shock* of your blow will penetrate into and/or through the target, depending upon where your mind is fixed.

Striking through the target extends your intention (referred to as *yi* in Chinese). Where your yi goes, your qi (vital energy) also goes. Yi and qi always travel together. Likewise, where your qi goes, your strength follows.

Chapter 6

Shorter Is Better

Parachutes and Punches

Why is it better to jump out of an airplane with a parachute than without one? I sure hope that you don't need more than a few seconds to answer this question! C'mon, put down that slice of pizza and think about it! What's the main difference between jumping with a parachute and jumping without one?

The answer has to do with time. When you jump with a parachute, assuming that you remember to pull the ripcord, it takes you a lot longer to land than it does if you jump without one. And if you understand that, then you also understand the *impulse-momentum change theorem*; a principle that is crucial to generating shock.

Impulse

Impulse is defined as a change in momentum. That is, it's the product of force acting on a body and the time over which that force is applied. This isn't nearly as complicated as it sounds. Consider:

- To effect a *large* change in momentum over a *long* period of time, only a *small force* is needed. When you pull the ripcord of your parachute the velocity of your fall suddenly decreases. This results in a large change in your momentum over a long period of time. Because you slow down, the force of your fall is reduced and your body won't leave a 2-foot impression in the ground.

■ To effect a *large* change in momentum in a *short* period of time, however, a much *larger force* is required. If you jump out of the airplane without the parachute, the velocity of your fall certainly won't decrease. But, as they say, "It isn't the fall that kills you—it's the sudden stop at the end." There's going to be large change in your momentum (and your consciousness), but it's going to happen in a microsecond and leave a real icky spot on the ground. The force involved in this scenario is considerably larger.

So, *the shorter the time the force is applied, the more powerful it is.* If you want to exert as much force as possible with your techniques, you must practice to minimize the time over which the force of your technique is in contact with the target.

Many contemporary martial art devotees have forgotten a very important principle that is central to the development of real power. It states:

The sharp power of a blow is inversely proportionate to the length of time it remains in contact with the target.

The longer the time your force is applied to the target, the less shock you will generate. In fact, you'll create more of a "push" than a sharp blow. If your punch or kick strikes your opponent too early, your elbow or knee will still be well bent at the time of impact. If you try to drive your fist or foot through the aggressor without impulse, you'll only succeed in shoving him backwards. This is because you're increasing the time that your force is applied to the opponent (Figures 6-1 and 6-2).

If you'd prefer to deliver a truly destructive blow, you must train so that your techniques are capable of generating a sharp, penetrating form of shock that will wreak havoc with the internal tissues of your opponent.

Just Passing Through

Mark Hachey, a senior practitioner of yiliquan kung-fu, provided his students with a very interesting demonstration of shock. He asked for a volunteer who would be willing to receive a sharp slap on the chest. As one of his pupils stepped forward, Sifu Hachey explained that he would simply slap the young man on the chest and that no substantial discomfort would be felt.

So saying, he opened his palm and smacked his student smartly on the pectoral muscle. The blow stung only slightly but within a few seconds, the skin alongside the student's scapula (shoulder blade) turned bright red. The power of the blow had passed through the young man's body, exiting out his back! Had the power of the slap been directed at an internal organ the results would have been very serious.

Jim Burgess, also a senior yiliquan practitioner, provided a similar demonstration. His student held a heavy telephone book wrapped in duct tape against his chest. Sifu Burgess extended his arm so that his fingertips just touched the protective phone book. When the receiver indicated that he was ready, Burgess closed his hand and fired a sudden punch from a distance of only three inches or so. The blast of power caused his student to drop the phone book and grimace in pain. Within a short time a dark bruise formed on the student's back, indicating that the power of the thrust had completely penetrated his body!

Figure 6-1   **Figure 6-2**

Of the four types of impact, only two are capable of producing shock: the *focused impact* and the *snap-back impact*. This is because the force that is generated by these forms of impact is in contact with the target for only a fraction of a second. The force generated by the other two types of impact, *piercing impact* and *smashing impact*, are in contact with the target for a much longer time.

Chapter 7

The Foothold

The Importance of the Foundation

The strongest skyscraper is only as strong as its foundation. The same thing is true of martial arts practitioners. You're in serious trouble if you're unable to maintain a balanced position or if your foundation is unable to withstand the reaction force of your own techniques.

Back in the "old days" the development of strong stances was of paramount importance. Students were often made to practice various foothold exercises for several years to ensure that they developed a stable base from which they could issue power. These training routines were not only tedious; they were often quite painful and many a wannabe kung-fu or karate master gave in and gave up. Those who stuck it out developed very strong postures that enabled them to generate uncanny power with their punches and kicks. As an old Okinawan karate master once told me, "Stance is one of the great secrets of karate but very few people ever practice it anymore."

What Is a Stance?

Stances are static positions. You move *from* one stance *into* another. All stances are intended to do one of two things:

To serve as a stable position from which you can move quickly, and

To serve as a stable platform from which you can launch techniques.

If we compare your striking or kicking technique to a bullet, your stance is the rifle from which it is fired. If you were going into battle, which would you rather carry—a rifle that's clean and in good condition or a rusty piece of junk? Would you want to carry a rifle with which you're unfamiliar? Wouldn't you want to thoroughly acquaint yourself with your rifle before you go into harm's way? Well, then, how familiar are you with the stances you use in your chosen martial art? Are they stable? Let's find out.

Inward Tension Stances

Don't look so confused! I thought you said you were familiar with your stances. You say you've never heard of stances using inward tension? Well, you're about to.

Inward tension stances are *short stances* such as the cat stance, hook stance, *sancai* (a fundamental stance common to xingyiquan, baguazhang, and yiliquan), and karate's *sanchin* stance (see Figures 7-1 to 7-4). In these stances the adductors (muscles of the inner thighs) are contracted to provide stability.

If you just "sit" in one of these stances without contracting the adductors, you can be easily pushed off-balance. That means that if you strike something from this relaxed posture, you'll only succeed in launching yourself backwards. Therefore, when you deliver a blow from a short stance, you must establish a solid foundation by strongly contracting the adductors and gripping the ground with your toes.

Moreover, quick and agile movement from a relaxed stance is simply not possible. If you anticipate having to move abruptly, you should "load" the stance by *slightly* contracting the inner thighs. This has the effect of placing your posture on a "hair trigger." But remember, if the adductors are tensed too powerfully you will be locked into position and unable to move swiftly.

Figure 7-1. Cat stance

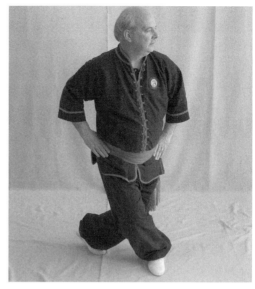

Figure 7-2. Hook stance

Figure 7-3. Sancai stance

Figure 7-4. Sanchin stance

Outward Tension Stances

If short stances use inward tension, what types of stances employ outward tension?

That's right, *long stances*. You're starting to catch on!

The forward stance, back stance, and horse-riding stance are all fine examples of stances that use outward tension. Although short stances allow for faster movement, long stances permit you to strike with greater power. This is because your knees are well bent and your feet are spread farther apart, thereby lowering your center of gravity. However, to take advantage of this larger power base, you must employ the appropriate *outward tension*.

The forward stance (which goes by various names, depending on which martial art you study) places most of the body's weight on the front leg. The rear leg should push down and back into the ground while the toes of the front foot "grab" the ground. The knee of the front leg should be directly over the toes (Figure 7-5).

Figure 7-5. Forward stance

Figure 7-6. Back stance

The back stance places just more than half of the body's weight on the rear leg, which is tensed outward. The toes of the front foot grasp the ground (Figure 7-6).

The horse-riding stance sets the body's weight evenly on both legs. The legs are tensed slightly outward as the toes of both feet dig into the ground (Figure 7-7).

Figure 7-7. Horse-riding stance

Sit Straight!

When you bend your knees and "sit" in your stance, it's important to sit straight.

Don't lean your upper body in any direction. If your upper body is tilted, your legs and hips have to work extra hard to keep you upright and the integrity of your stance is compromised (Figures 7-8 and 7-9).

Don't let your buttocks protrude out behind you (Figure 7-10). Even if you have a nice *derrière* your opponent probably won't be

Figure 7-8   **Figure 7-9**   **Figure 7-10**

impressed, so tuck it in and keep it to yourself. And anyway, when you stand like that your legs (specifically, the quadriceps muscles on the fronts of the thighs) have to work extra hard to keep you upright. You're unstable and you won't be able to generate much power.

Ideally, the lower part of your weighted leg (from the knee to the ankle) should be as vertical as possible. Your weight will then be centered directly over the spot on the bottom of the foot known as the *yongquan* point (Figure 7-11).

In the Chinese martial arts it is believed that it is through this point that the practitioner draws energy from, and roots himself to, the earth. It is also at this particular area of the sole of the foot where humans naturally balance themselves. If the majority of your weight is placed over this point, you're able to maintain a stable

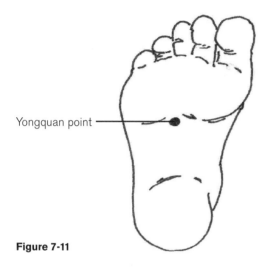

Yongquan point

Figure 7-11

Figure 7-12

Figure 7-13

Figure 7-14

position with minimal effort. Conversely, the farther the leg drifts from the perpendicular, the less stable the stance becomes (Figures 7-12 to 7-14).

Overextension of Muscles and Joints

Contemporary *wushu* is a popular performing art that is an amalgamation of gymnastics, Chinese opera, and martial arts postures. Its practitioners often dramatize their performances with very deep and extended postures, which, although they are aesthetically pleasing, contain very little real power. Why? It's because:

A muscle produces power only when it contracts.

Therefore, a muscle that is fully extended is weak. If it doesn't contract it's unable to produce any power. So, if the rear leg of a forward stance is stretched out and the knee is locked straight, the rear foot cannot be pressed against the floor and produce the striking

power that is required for the delivery of a truly powerful blow (Figure 7-15). This is why practitioners of most traditional martial arts never lock the knee of the rear leg.

The driving foot presses against the ground for only a split second, so that the time that the striking force is applied (to the opponent's vital point) is minimized as much as possible. This is not nearly as easy to do as it sounds. Go ahead and try it. And if you have no idea what I'm talking about, you need to contact a memory therapist before going back and re-reading Chapter 6.

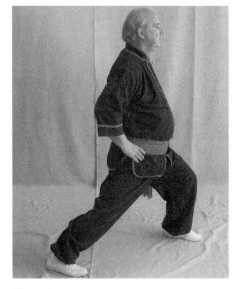

Figure 7-15

Figure 7-16

Training with deep stances can be beneficial insofar as the development of strength in the hips and legs is concerned, but deep stances have very little value in actual combat. In order to move quickly and powerfully, the muscles of the legs and hips must be able to contract very abruptly and lift the weight of the body. If the stance is overextended or excessively deep, the muscles cannot contract quickly enough to facilitate fast, strong movement.

Also, placing too much stress on the knees will eventually have detrimental effects. It is far more efficient to stand with the buttocks higher than the knees (Figure 7-16).

Chapter 8

The Importance of Footwork

Although you may develop a thunderbolt punch or an earth-shattering kick, it's of no value if you can't strike your opponent with it. To be able to do that you have to master stance and footwork, twin subjects that are often eschewed by beginning students who would rather spend their time trying to beat the stuffing out of the heavy bag. Remember that heavy bags don't try to evade you or strike back. Opponents do. So, if you want to be able to effectively apply your techniques in actual combat, you must first learn how to stand and move.

What Is Footwork?

The various stepping techniques of martial arts (referred to as *bufa* in Chinese) serve two fundamental purposes. They:

- Enable you to evade the enemy's attack, and
- Allow you to move close enough to the opponent so that you can effectively apply your own techniques

In a basic sense, footwork is what happens *between* stances. Some martial arts such as baguazhang and yiliquan stress the importance of evading the opponent's attacks and place great emphasis on the practice of various forms of bufa. However, simply practicing the individual stepping techniques is not enough. You must be able to move the entire body as an integrated unit, with speed and fluidity while maintaining perfect balance. The only way to accomplish this is to learn to *move from your dantien*.

What Is the Dantien?

The *dantien* (in Japanese, *tanden*) is located roughly three finger-widths below the navel and about two finger-widths inside. Although some teachers infer that it is an actual point on the surface of the

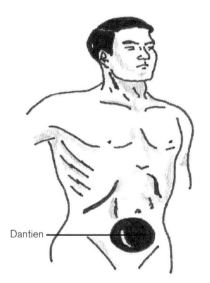

skin, it is actually more like a ball that fills up most of the lower abdomen (Figure 8-1).

This is where the body's vital energy (qi or ki) accumulates, and it is from the dantien that the life force flows out to nourish and energize the entire body (into and through the acupuncture channels).

Discussing the fundamental theories of traditional Chinese medicine is beyond the scope of this book and it really doesn't matter whether you believe in the concept of qi. What is important is that you understand that the dantien is the physical center of a human body and that all movement must originate from there.

Dantien

Figure 8-1

Striking the Wind

My teacher, Mr. W. C. Chen, was trying to explain the importance of moving the body as a unified whole. He wasn't having much success. My classmates and I couldn't really understand what he wanted us to do or why it was so important. Frustrated almost beyond words, Chen grumbled and told me to square off in my fighting stance. "You attack me as fast as you can," he said. "Hit me! Punch, kick, whatever you want to do."

As I brought my hands up, Chen stood comfortably with his hands at his sides not more than 4 feet in front of me. He was relaxed but I felt his eyes boring into my soul.

Oh, boy . . . every time he does something like this, I get whacked! Ah, well. . . .

I went into a full-volume rock 'n roll mode and drove forward, firing my best punch straight at his chin.

But he wasn't there. He had seemingly vanished, and instead of being in front of me, he was standing right *beside* me! I smiled. He didn't.

How'd he do that?

"Try again," Chen instructed. "Really try this time. Please!"

I relaxed, breathing down into my abdomen. My classmates had always told me that my front kick was very fast—so fast that they were rarely able to evade it. I decided that I'd blast him with my best front kick.

And I tried. I really did. But just before my foot should have struck him squarely in the belly I noticed that Chen was standing beside me again, glaring.

"Now I attack," Chen said. "You defend, okay?"

"Yes, sir," I answered.

(continued on next page)

I hope this doesn't hurt too bad.

I stepped back and brought my hands up in an on-guard position. By the time I saw Chen's movement his fist was almost touching the tip of my nose.

"You did not defend," he chided me. "Please defend."

Well, it's not like I didn't plan on it!

We squared off again. I thought I saw the old man slightly shift his weight, but by the time I began to deflect his attack, it was already finished. He stood in front of me, having quickly withdrawn his fist to avoid punching a large hole in my face.

"You must learn to move from here," Chen said, as he patted his lower belly. "Then the whole body moves at the same time. It makes my movement very fast, very strong. You are not moving in this way. When you attack, your head moves first and I know you are coming. Your movement is too slow and very weak. You hit only the air. I move my whole body all at once. By the time you see that I am coming, I am already there! If I attack, you cannot defend."

And with that, Chen began teaching us how to move from the dantien. This time around we paid close attention and learned. So, if you'd like to be able to do what Chen did, pay heed to my words.

How to Move from the Dantien

To move your whole body as an integrated unit, you must move from the center of your body. If you do otherwise you will begin your movement by leaning or shifting individual parts of the upper or lower body. Such movements lack a solid foundation. They are disjointed, unbalanced, and weak. In the classical internal martial arts, the extremities never move independently of the rest of the body; they move in conjunction with the dantien. In this way the integrity of the whole body is maintained and great power can be manifested.

I teach students how to walk from the dantien in the earliest stages of their training. Presented here are a couple of basic exercises that clearly demonstrate the efficiency of this kind of movement:

■ Exercise: Walking from Your Dantien

Have a partner stand several yards in front of you with one arm outstretched, and walk toward him naturally. He will tense his arm and try to stop your forward movement as you walk into his hand. Don't cheat and lean into him. Keep your back straight and walk normally. The odds are that you'll be stopped dead in your tracks when your chest comes in contact with his hand (Figures 8-2 and 8-3).

Figure 8-2   Figure 8-3

Figure 8-4

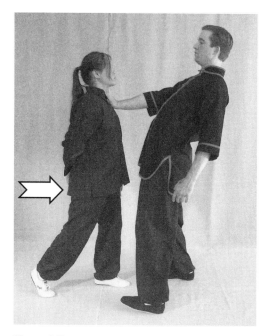

Figure 8-5

The reason your partner is able to halt your movement with minimal effort is because your body parts are not moving together even though they're physically connected. All he has to do is stop your isolated pectoral muscle and the rest of your body will likewise come to a halt. He can use the combined strength of his upper back, chest (pectoral muscle), and arm against the strength of your lone pectoral muscle! Not much of a contest, is it?

As you begin again, place the back of one hand against the end of your coccyx (Figure 8-4).

Don't be shy about touching the coccyx; it's yours. When you advance, give a slight push with your hand as though pushing outward through your dantien. Slightly contract the anal sphincter. This helps unify your lower and upper body. When you walk into your partner's hand you will be able to easily move him backward and continue to advance. Be sure that you don't lean forward. Keep your spine and neck aligned as you push forward on your coccyx (Figure 8-5).

This is what the Taijiquan Classics mean when they speak of "moving forward through the back." You can also practice walking backwards using this same technique. Simply place the palm of one hand on your dantien and push backwards slightly as you retreat (Figure 8-6).

(Note: The Taijiquan Classics are a collection of early writings about the art. These teachings, most of which were written by members of the Yang family, have been used as a standard by *neijia* stylists for nearly 200 years.)

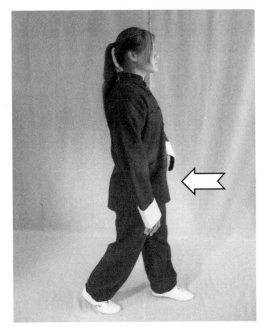

Figure 8-6

■ Exercise: Moving between Stances from Your Dantien

Once you have learned how to move from your dantien while walking, you must learn to do it as you move from one stance to another. It's important that you learn to move your entire body—from your crown to the soles of your feet—as a single unit.

If you have a full-length mirror you can watch yourself and ensure that you're moving your whole body as an integrated unit. If you don't have a large mirror, concentrate on feeling your movements.

Begin in a forward stance. As you advance your rear foot a full step, watch and feel your body's movement. If you're not moving from your dantien you'll probably notice that your upper body tends to lean slightly forward before you actually advance your foot (Figures 8-7 and 8-8).

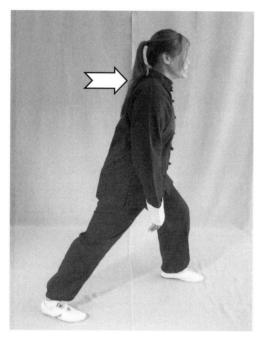

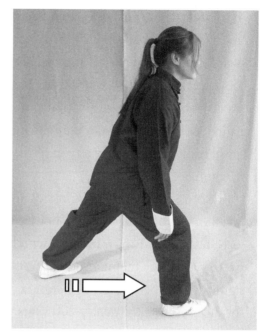

Figure 8-7

Figure 8-8

Now place the back of one hand on the tip of your coccyx, as before. As you begin to advance, push forward with the back of your hand and feel the force moving straight through your dantien.

When you move, slightly contract the anal sphincter and ensure that the coccyx is tucked slightly forward. This will help you move correctly, and if you begin to lean you'll be able to feel it. Your balance will be greatly enhanced and your movement will be much more powerful (Figures 8-9 and 8-10).

This training drill can also be practiced with a partner in the same manner as the walking exercise above (Figure 8-11).

Figure 8-9

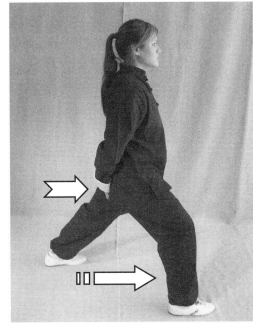

Figure 8-10

Figure 8-11

Common Errors

Many students tend to watch their feet as they learn to move from the dantien. This is a serious error for two reasons.

- *Watching your feet as you move compromises the proper alignment of the spine,* which destabilizes your stance and weakens your movement.

- *When you look down, it acts as a sort of brake.* Your body wants to come to a halt but you're forcing it to move. If we liken it to driving a car, it's like stepping on the accelerator and the brake pedal at the same time.

Moving from the Dantien in Everyday Life

Moving from your dantien must become an unconscious habit. It has to become the way in which you normally move and this can be achieved only through regular practice over a period of time. Although walking with your hand on your coccyx is an excellent way to practice these exercises at home or in the training hall, it's a quick and sure form of professional and social suicide if you do it at work or when you're out on the town!

Nonetheless, you should check yourself several times throughout the day to ensure that you are moving from your dantien. This is easy to do if you've been paying attention to how it feels. If you find that you are not moving correctly, you can use one finger to press lightly on your dantien as a gentle reminder. It's important to learn to make every movement from your One-Point (another term for the dantien), whether it's sitting down, standing up, walking, running, or any other movement. Moving in this way allows you to move very powerfully and with minimal physical stress.

Most people tend to bounce or sway when they walk or run. The old adage that tells you to "walk with a spring in your step" is actually a terrible piece of advice. Consider what happens when you adhere to this asinine admonition. First, one leg must literally toss your body's weight into the air. If you weigh, say, 180 pounds, that's quite an effort! The other leg must catch that weight to prevent you from crashing to the ground and then toss it up and forward again so that you can take another step.

You couldn't do this with your arms because they're not nearly strong enough to toss and catch 180 pounds repeatedly, but your legs and hips are very durable and they'll do it … for a while. Eventually, they begin to weaken and you experience pain in your ankles, knees, hips, and/or lower back. If you persist in walking in this manner, you may eventually damage certain bones, ligaments, and muscles.

However, when you move from your dantien, your hips don't bounce. They *glide* along an even plane. The legs never have to catch or toss your weight; all they have to do is push about 50 percent of your body weight at any one time. This is akin to rolling a large ball rather than throwing it into the air and catching it. The ankles, knees, hips, and lower back aren't excessively stressed and the body's movements are better balanced, smoother, and faster. In modern society, where we spend much of our lives standing, walking, or running on concrete or asphalt, this is an important consideration.

Chapter 9

Using the Body as a Fist

Lions and Tigers and Bears!

For hundreds of years man has sought to advance his combative skills by emulating the fighting tactics employed by various creatures. For instance, the tiger prefers to approach its prey from the flank and then strike suddenly from its victim's "blind side." Cranes use their wings to beat at and distract the enemy before they attack with their beaks and claws. The bear is renowned for its enormous strength, lions and tigers are revered for their agility and ferocity, and the snake is famous for its one-pointed concentration and blinding speed.

Some martial arts strive to actually imitate the physical movements of certain animals, and it is my contention that this kind of mimicry is seriously flawed. For instance, tigers can generate enormous power by striking from the outside inward with their front legs and claws, but they cannot lift a very heavy weight with their paws nor can they generate much power by striking from the inside outward. This is because they have free-floating clavicles that do not articulate with the other bones as they do in humans. Our distinctive human structure allows us to lift heavy objects and strike in a wide variety of directions—things that cats and snakes cannot do.

When a snake strikes, it hurls itself at its prey. It has no control over itself once the attack is initiated. The same is true of the praying mantis. Monkeys possess enormous upper-body strength, which is essential to their survival as tree dwellers. Birds such as cranes and eagles have hollow bones that make them light enough for flight.

You are not a tree dweller, nor can you fly. No matter how much you may practice or fantasize about it, you will never develop the great strength of the monkey, the lightness and agility of the crane, or the blinding speed of the mantis. You aren't built like these creatures and you'll never be able to move as they do. You're a human being and you move like a human being. It is therefore essential to learn how to make the best use of your uniquely human structure.

The Eight Body Actions

Any movement we make will create *force* but there are only eight ways in which a human body can move and create *shock*. I refer to these as the *eight body actions*. They are the ways in which we utilize the laws of physics and kinesiology to increase the efficiency of our techniques by maximizing the mass used in each technique and moving it at the highest possible velocity. This is achieved by learning to move the dantien in a variety of ways.

It is crucial that you learn to strike and kick with the strength of your whole body rather than just your arm or leg. The isolated strength of an individual limb is incapable of producing much power. On the other hand, striking with the force of the entire body produces astonishing power due to an increase in mass.

We'll look at the following eight body actions, one at a time:

- Body rotation
- Body throw
- Body up
- Body circle
- Body shift
- Body vibration
- Body down
- Body whip

Body Rotation

This is the first and most fundamental body action taught to new trainees because it's natural and easy to perform. In fact, it's very much like the body action involved in throwing a baseball.

The object is to turn the hips and waist 45 degrees as quickly as possible.

1. Begin in a forward stance with the navel turned inward 45 degrees and the leading arm extended. The rear fist is chambered for a punch. The upper body is relaxed and the rear leg is slightly flexed (Figure 9-1).

Figure 9-1

2. Contract the anal sphincter as you squeeze your buttocks together and drive the rear foot and leg against the ground like a piston. This will snap your rear hip around so that your navel points directly forward as you execute a thrust with the rear fist (Figure 9-2). Keep the forward knee pointed at the target.

Punching in this way is often referred to as a *reverse punch* because the punch is delivered with the rear (reverse) fist.

It isn't just the rotation of the hips and waist that produces shock; it's how *quickly* you can do it! The faster you can do it, the better. You must also utilize reverse breathing as you move (see Chapter 10). The faster you exhale, the faster you will move. Exhale two-thirds of

Figure 9-2

Figure 9-3

Figure 9-4

your breath as quickly as possible as you execute your technique. Always keep one-third of your breath in reserve.

Reverse rotation involves rotating the forward hip 45 degrees. It's often used in delivering techniques such as the jab or the horizontal sword-hand strike. It is performed as follows.

1. Begin in a forward stance, but with the navel pointed straight ahead (Figure 9-3). The rear hand is extended forward and the leading arm is chambered back in preparation for a sword-hand strike.

2. Press down with your front foot and snap the leading hip forward to turn the navel inward 45 degrees as you strike outward with your leading hand. Do not allow the forward leg to straighten out and make sure that your hips don't rise up. Keep the rear leg flexed and perform this body movement through the pressure of your foot on the ground. As in rotation, the lower body does not move much at all (Figure 9-4).

Rotation and *reverse rotation* are used in executing many of the upper-body techniques and several kicking techniques, such as the round-house kick.

Common Errors

■ *Don't rotate the hips too far*, as shown in Figure 9-5, and *don't begin with the navel pointing 90 degrees from the target*, as shown in Figure 9-6. A rotation of more than 45 degrees is too large and will produce a pushing effect rather than engendering shock.

Figure 9-5

Figure 9-6

■ *Be careful not to contract the abdominal muscles inward.* This exaggerated form of normal breathing will prevent you from using the integrated strength of your upper and lower body because it separates and isolates them.

■ *Don't raise the heel of your rear foot* (Figure 9-7). If you can't recollect why, go back and re-read the Common Errors section of Chapter 5.

■ *Don't straighten your rear leg.* Remember what I said about that in Chapter 7? You've got to pay attention because all of this stuff dovetails.

Figure 9-7

■ *Be careful that your front knee doesn't wobble.* If it does, your stability will be compromised and you can kiss your power goodbye.

Body Shift

This body action is used almost exclusively for kicking. The idea is to shift your hips and dantien directly toward the target. Some slight rotation of the hips is often involved as well.

In performing the front snap kick, the supporting foot (which is also your driving foot) presses against the ground as the hips are thrust slightly forward, toward the target. The hip of the kicking leg will rotate forward as well (Figure 9-8).

The front thrust kick uses a stronger thrust of the hips. You must not kick with the strength of the leg alone. Kick with your whole body! (See Figure 9-9.)

Figure 9-8

Figure 9-9

In the side thrust kick, the hip is thrust out to the side and may include some rotation (Figure 9-10).

The back thrust kick involves a slight backward thrust of the hips (Figure 9-11).

Figure 9-10   **Figure 9-11**

Common Errors

- Be careful that you *don't shift your hips too far in the direction of the kick*. This will cause your upper body, which comprises a very large portion of your body's mass, to lean away from the kick. The end result will be that you'll knock yourself backwards with the force of your own kick! (See Figures 9-12 and 9-13.)

Figure 9-12   **Figure 9-13**

- *Try to keep your head as upright as possible.* Your body tends to follow your head. If you tilt your head backward, your body will follow, and you may end up on the floor trying to remember your name.
- Unless you're trying out for the cheerleading squad, *never, ever rise up on the ball of your supporting foot when you perform a kick.* It may look pretty and enable you to kick higher, but if you ever kick an opponent like that the resultant reaction force will cause you to lose your balance, possibly some teeth, and the fight.

Body Throw

This body action is used for delivering lunging thrusts. It is generally considered to be the most powerful body action because it moves more of your mass than any of the other body actions. Most percussive martial arts practice some form of lunging punch, but it is seldom seen in freestyle sparring. If you ask why this is so, you will probably be told that this type of movement is simply too slow or too awkward for use in actual fighting.

Nonsense!

Everything in traditional martial arts exists for a reason. If you can't execute this movement fast enough to use it effectively in sparring, it's probably because you're doing it wrong. So, pay attention.

1. Begin in a forward stance with the leading arm and fist extended (Figure 9-14).
2. Quickly contract the adductors (the muscles of the inner thighs) in a squeezing action to bring the rear leg forward as quickly as possible (Figure 9-15).

    You must move from your dantien as if someone is pushing on your sacrum and coccyx. And, remember, *maintain spinal alignment.*

Figure 9-14

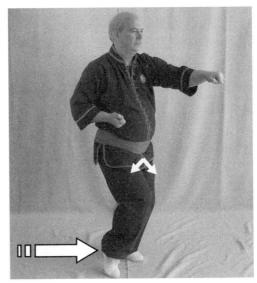

Figure 9-15

3. Relax the adductors as you drive your rear foot against the ground and deliver a lunging punch. The striking hip should rotate 45 degrees forward when you execute your thrust or strike (Figure 9-16).

Don't try to "think through" each stage of this movement. That'll just inhibit your movement. Simply *squeeze-drive!* Turn these actions into a single, seamless movement.

Coordinate the movement of your body with an explosive exhalation, using a reverse breath (see Chapter 10). Make

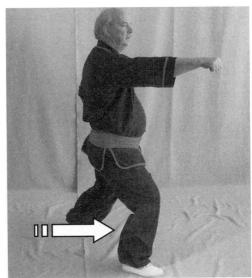

Figure 9-16

sure that you begin your exhalation at the beginning of the movement since that's where you need the greatest blast of power. You

Figure 9-17

must overcome your body's initial resistance to movement (inertia) and drive it forward in a balanced, controlled manner. With practice this maneuver can be executed with surprising speed.

Common Errors

- *Don't lean forward even slightly.* This is sometimes called "leading with your face."
- *Avoid raising the heel of your rear foot* (Figure 9-17).
- *Don't look down.* Remember, looking down "slams on the brakes."

Figure 9-18

Body Vibration

The body action of *vibration* is used only in the execution of snap-back impact techniques such as the back fist strikes. Most martial arts adepts simply lob these strikes at their opponents, using only the power of the arm and shoulder. However, by learning to employ body vibration you will be able to deliver a lightning-fast strike that utilizes the power of your entire body.

1. Begin in a forward stance with the forward elbow and navel pointing toward the target as if in preparation for a horizontal back fist strike (Figure 9-18).
2. As the strike begins and the fist travels to the target, the leading hip rotates forward (using reverse rotation) about 30 degrees.
3. At the instant after impact, the leading hip snaps back to the beginning position and the fist and forearm snap back to the original position. Emphasis is on the sudden and powerful backward rotation of the hip. (See Figures 9-19 and 9-20.)

Figure 9-19

Figure 9-20

Take your time and learn to perform this movement correctly, gradually building speed as you become more comfortable with it. When the movement is done correctly and quickly, the hips appear to vibrate.

Common Errors

Beginning students often have difficulty learning to execute this body action because they *rotate the striking hip too far forward, rotate the wrong hip forward, or stick the hip out to one side* (Figures 9-21 and 9-22).

Figure 9-21

Figure 9-22

Body Up

The body action of *up* is used for strikes or thrusts that travel upward, such as the *zuanquan* (uppercut punch) of xingyiquan.

1. Begin in a forward stance but lower the hips slightly more than usual.

2. As you strike or thrust upward, let the hips rise straight up (Figures 9-23 and 9-24).

Figure 9-23

Figure 9-24

Common Errors

- *Do not straighten the legs or stretch upward*, as this will destabilize you and actually reduce striking power (Figure 9-25). The upward movement is really very slight.

- *Don't raise your chin*, as that will compromise the alignment of your vertebrae and weaken your posture.

Figure 9-25

Body Down

The body action of *down* is used for strikes that are delivered in a descending manner.

1. Begin in a normal forward stance.
2. As you strike downward, lower the hips slightly and sink straight down by bending the knees (Figures 9-26 and 9-27).

Figure 9-26   **Figure 9-27**

Figure 9-28

Common Errors

- *Do not bend over at the waist*, as this will result in a loss of striking power as well as balance (Figure 9-28).
- *Don't jump up and then come crashing down on your target*. This kind of movement relies entirely on momentum. Although it may enable you to break a few brittle bricks

in exhibitions, it's an extremely slow and risky movement to attempt in a serious altercation.

Body Circle

The action of *circling* is used for executing various throwing techniques, or to deliver a strike with the hips. It is executed to the sides.

The dantien is rolled upward slightly to one side as the hip thrusts slightly outward (Figure 9-29).

Remember, the dantien is like a ball that can roll or turn in any direction.

Figure 9-29

Body Whip

The body action of a *whip* (also known as "dragon's back") is used for executing various thrusting techniques.

1. Withdraw the shoulders as if trying to touch the shoulder blades together (Figure 9-30).
2. Thrust the hips and dantien forward to create a wave-like effect through the spine. This action is transmitted to the shoulders, which drive slightly forward as the thrust is made (Figures 9-31 and 9-32).

Figure 9-30

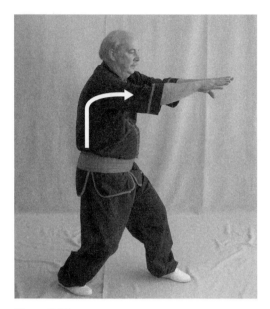

Figure 9-31

Figure 9-32

Figure 9-33

When you strike with one hand and utilize the body action of the whip, the basic body action of rotation is also involved. The striking hip rotates forward 45 degrees as the spine whips forward. Figure 9-33 illustrates xingyiquan's posture of *piquan* (which usually strikes with the outer edge of the palm) using the body action of the whip.

Chapter 10

The Secrets of Breathing

Breathing and the Martial Arts

Beginning students usually show minimal interest in practicing special breathing techniques. They want to get into the "meat" of the matter and learn how to punch, kick, and practice fighting drills. They don't understand that correct breathing is essential to the effective execution and application of all techniques. An old Shao-lin saying tells us:

He who knows strength also knows breathing.

In this regard we are talking about *real* strength instead of what looks like strength. So, don't just skim through this chapter, because it actually contains some of the most important information in the entire book.

The special breathing techniques used in the practice of traditional martial arts were not always taught openly. Many teachers jealously guarded this knowledge because it gave them a very real advantage over anyone with whom they crossed fists or swords. However, with the passage of time these arcane techniques were ultimately divulged and taught openly within many combative disciplines.

Unfortunately, within a few generations many martial arts practitioners abandoned this great treasure. They disliked the practice of tedious breathing exercises. Instead, they concentrated on practicing the more exciting physical techniques of punching, kicking, and cutting. The special breathing techniques that were once considered an essential aspect of training were neglected and eventually forgotten altogether.

Fortunately for us, a dedicated few continued to practice these obscure exercises and the ancient teachings were preserved. This is how these techniques have come to be "secrets" once again; they've been remembered by only a few!

Karate styles such as Goju-ryu and Uechi-ryu as well as numerous forms of kung-fu emphasize the importance of learning how to breathe properly. After all, breathing affects every aspect of our lives. Stability, speed, balance, body unity, and health maintenance are all strongly affected and enhanced by correct breathing.

Breathing and Stability

Whenever you execute a technique—whether it's a punch, a kick, or a grappling technique—breath control plays a key role. It provides for the stability of the body, and the speed and power of the technique. Without these important ingredients, technique amounts to little more than flailing your arms or legs in the air.

You know that a stable foundation is absolutely essential for the execution of powerful techniques, right? Without a solid root, even the strongest man in the world is rendered helpless. Correct breathing ensures that balance is maintained throughout the execution of your technique. It stabilizes your stance and roots you to the ground.

Lowering your center of gravity enhances your stability so that your techniques can be delivered with greater force. However, many martial arts enthusiasts seem to adhere to the "more is better" philosophy. They hunker down so low that they look like they're trying to use a "squatter" in a third-world country! This is not only foolish and unnecessary; it is dangerous insofar as training for actual combat is concerned (I'm referring to standing with your stance too low, not using a squatter … although that can also be risky). Sinking the stance slightly can enhance your stability to some degree but the buttocks should never be level with, nor lower than, your knees.

There's no need to lower your stance to ridiculous levels in order to sink your center of gravity; the same thing can be accomplished through correct breathing. In fact, proper breathing technique will enable you to drop your center of gravity below ground level! This is the true meaning of "being rooted." Roots grow

Figure 10-1

beneath the ground, not above it. If your stance is truly rooted, your center of gravity falls below ground level and provides a very stable base from which you can issue extremely powerful techniques (Figure 10-1).

Breathing and Speed

If we compare the execution of a percussive technique to the eruptive discharge of a firearm, the fist or foot is the bullet and the breath is the gunpowder that propels it. Without the explosive power of the gunpowder, the bullet is as useless as a pebble.

Some students let out a little squeak when they strike. This can be likened to the firing of a small .22-caliber bullet. In many traditional martial arts the exhalation is much more explosive and can be likened to firing a much larger round. Their techniques can be so terribly destructive that a single blow may be enough to end the conflict.

The human body acts like a machine that is powered by a bellows. The greater the volume of air pumped through it, the more strength the body can generate. And the *faster* the air is pumped through it, the *faster* the body will move. This is why we emphasize that you must exhale two-thirds of your breath in the space of a gunshot. BANG, and it's over! Two-thirds of your breath is expelled almost instantly!

Remember that speed is power. The .223-caliber bullet is really just a .22 round backed up with a large powder charge. It travels at extremely high velocity and, although it is smaller than many other rifle bullets, it is capable of inflicting tremendous damage on its target because it produces hydrostatic shock upon impact. If you want your technique (the bullet) to travel at extremely high velocity so as to produce maximum destructive power, you must train your breath (the gunpowder).

Breathing and Body Unity

Besides providing greater stability and increasing the velocity of your techniques, the breath is also used to accommodate another physical law. This one says that the more mass we can bring into the execution of a technique, the stronger it will be ($F = ma$, remember?).

Correct breathing strengthens certain muscle connections that run between the upper and lower body. This allows us to utilize the strength and mass of the entire body rather than just the power of the individual limbs.

Breathing and Health Maintenance

We all know that breathing is essential for sustaining life. However, the air we breathe not only provides us with the necessary physical components (such as oxygen) needed to sustain life, but also qi (internal energy).

I believe that one of the things that contributes to the aging process and the accompanying decline in overall health is the failure to breathe correctly. Several ancient exercise regimens such as the ancient *baduanjin* ("Eight Pieces of Brocade") use the breath to massage the viscera and other internal tissues to keep them in optimum working order.

Breathing and Vulnerability

Breathing also plays a key role in determining when you and your opponent are most vulnerable to sudden attack. During inhalation and, to a lesser degree, any time the breath is paused, a person's reaction time is lengthened and his ability to resist force is considerably reduced. This is very important information for martial arts practitioners; you must always strive to strike the enemy when he is inhaling or when his breath is paused! This will require very sharp timing and loads of practice.

At the same time, you must learn to "hide your breath" so the enemy cannot easily determine when you are most vulnerable. This isn't easy to do, especially when the heat is on, the chips are down, and you're sucking wind. However, if you train yourself to utilize reverse breathing (see the next section) under stressful conditions, you'll be able to stabilize your breath very quickly.

Basic Forms of Breathing

In the traditional Chinese internal arts, three forms of breathing are taught: normal breathing, reverse breathing, and inverse breathing. In this chapter, we will discuss the first two forms of breathing. Inverse breathing is taught only to advanced students and will be presented in a future volume.

Normal versus Reverse Breathing

Many present-day martial arts schools utilize what is known as *normal breathing*. This is the way most people breathe—thus the name. In normal breathing the lower abdomen expands slightly upon inhalation and then contracts during exhalation (Figures 10-2 and 10-3). When martial arts practitioners utilize this form of breathing, they exhale through the mouth and strongly contract the abdominal muscles. Is this what you do? If it is, stop doing it!

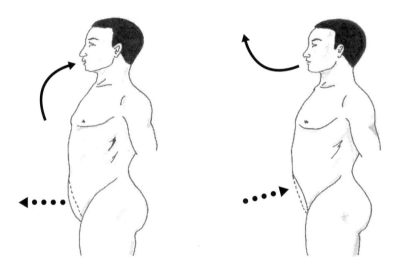

Figure 10-2   **Figure 10-3**

Normal breathing actually weakens your technique because the contraction of the abdominals acts to undermine the muscle connections that run between the upper and lower body. The strength of the upper body is separated from that of the lower body, and you become like a doughnut. You have strength in the extremities but nothing in the middle. Normal breathing denies you the use of the power of the dantien and the full strength of the muscles of the abdomen and lower back.

Reverse breathing is one of the secrets of the internal martial arts, although it was once commonly employed by many external arts as well. This unique breathing technique moves the abdomen in a manner opposite to that used in normal breathing—thus its name. Reverse breathing strengthens the muscle connections between the upper and lower body so that the power of the entire body can be concentrated in any given movement.

How to Perform Reverse Breathing

To perform the reverse breath:

1. Inhale through your nose and slightly *contract* the abdomen. Don't expand your chest or raise your shoulders (Figure 10-4).

2. As you exhale through your mouth, *expand* the lower abdomen, along with the front, sides, and lower back, outward (Figure 10-5). Slightly contract the anal sphincter and tuck the coccyx forward and upward.

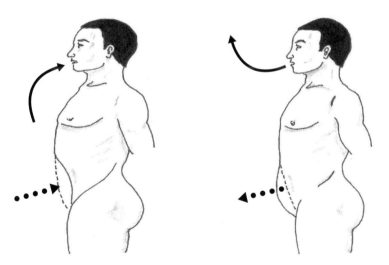

Figure 10-4   **Figure 10-5**

The chest must not be arched out as this will pull the diaphragm upward and prevent you from "pushing" your breath down as you exhale. This is why the internal styles of martial arts, as well as many external forms, stress the importance of slightly collapsing the chest, dropping the shoulders, and rounding out the upper back. If you adhere to these simple points, you will easily be able to "drop" your breath down as you exhale.

Reverse Breathing and Strength

Reverse breathing is not restricted to the application of martial arts technique. Any time you need to exert strength—for lifting, pushing, or pulling a heavy object, for example—you can use reverse breathing to increase your strength. Your physical power will be doubled (at the very least) the first time you try it.

When you are exerting a lot of physical strength, you should exhale slowly, in accordance with the speed of your movement.

To Serve and Protect

Reverse breathing is also part of the first stage of developing the legendary *iron shirt*, which is a special technique that utilizes one's vital energy (qi) to protect the body. After you have practiced reverse breathing for a year or so, you will find that whenever you exhale your body is highly resistant to an opponent's blows. This is because reverse breathing stimulates the flow of energy in the (acupuncture) channels and all of the internal tissues of the body.

Additionally, reverse breathing generates a strong flow of qi even though you may not have necessarily practiced any special forms of *qigong* on a regular basis. Try the simple experiments described here, as exercises.

■ Exercise: Immovable Posture

Stand naturally with your arms hanging at your sides. Your partner should stand behind you and place his hands in your armpits. Have him lift you straight up so that he can get the feel of your true weight. Make sure he lifts with his legs and that he does not cause you to lose your balance.

When he tries to lift you a second time, exhale powerfully using reverse breathing. You will find that this simple technique dramatically increases your ability to root yourself to the ground (Figure 10-6).

Figure 10-6

■ Exercise: Resisting Strikes

Stand in a horse-riding stance. Let your partner use his forearm to strike against your abdomen as you perform a strong reverse breath (Figure 10-7). You will find that his blows tend to bounce off with little or no discomfort and you are easily able to maintain your balance. Begin with light blows, and then, over a period of weeks and months, allow your partner to gradually increase the power of his blows.

Figure 10-7

Stabilizing the Breath and the Mind

When you have strongly exerted yourself and you're sucking air, you can easily and quickly stabilize your breathing rhythm by performing three or four reverse breaths slowly and forcefully.

When you're feeling mentally stressed, confused, or frightened, take time to perform several long, robust reverse breaths. You'll feel calmer, more relaxed, and better able to focus your mind on the task at hand.

The Real Function of the Belt

Did you know that the belt or sash that you wrap around your waist when you don your karate or kung-fu uniform actually has a specific training function? Before they were used to delineate rank, belts and sashes were worn to assist students in learning how to breathe properly.

When they exhaled with a forceful reverse breath, trainees could feel the abdomen expand and push against the belt or sash that was wrapped firmly around the waist. Karate practitioners often set the knot of the karate *obi* (belt) directly over the dantien to further enhance this sensation. Kung-fu stylists frequently wore a thin cotton belt underneath their street clothes for the same reason.

The Real Meaning of Balance

The ability to firmly root yourself is a good measure of your real martial prowess. No amount of running or weightlifting will be of any use in developing this special skill. Only repeated, regular practice of correct breathing will cultivate it. Without a firm root your techniques will have no real power and your movements will be unbalanced, awkward, and flimsy.

It all has to do with balance. In the traditional martial arts the word "balance" refers not only to physical balance, but also to mental stability. The former refers to the equilibrium of the body while the latter refers to the equilibrium of the mind. If you stumble or wobble, we would say that you have lost your physical balance. If you become very confused, extremely fearful, panicky, or hysterical, we would say that your mental balance has gone awry.

These two forms of balance are interrelated and interdependent. Loss of one inevitably leads to loss of the other. For instance, when you stumble and begin to fall, you become fearful. This is an example of how loss of physical balance causes loss of mental balance. If you become suddenly frightened, your legs may become weak and your whole body feels drained. This is an example of how loss of mental balance results in a loss of physical balance.

When one type of balance is maintained, the other form is likewise upheld. For instance, when you are physically stable and feel that you are standing upon a firm foundation, your mind is clear and your spirit is calm. When you feel self-assured and mentally secure, your body is also firmly balanced and your movements are sure and strong.

The Relationship between Breathing and Balance

Physical and mental balance are lost or maintained together, and both conditions—loss of physical balance and loss of mental balance—are always accompanied by *loss of breath!*

When you gasp for breath, when your breathing is shallow and high in the chest, your balance is easily lost. For instance, you probably gasp for breath when you stumble and begin to fall. When you're suddenly frightened or surprised, you do the same thing. This loss of correct breathing cuts off your ability to maintain a firm root and maintain proper balance of both body and mind.

Years ago, a study of this phenomenon was made by several psychologists. They determined that mental states such as panic and hysteria were always accompanied by shallow, high breathing. They found that when breathing is kept low in the abdomen, it is not physiologically possible to become hysterical or panic-stricken! In traditional martial arts students are taught to perform a strong reverse breath if they feel that they are about to lose either their physical or mental balance. Breathing in this way will help you maintain your balance and, even if your balance has already been lost, it can be quickly re-acquired by performing this simple breathing technique.

Training the Breath and Balance Together

The relationship between balance and breath was once common knowledge throughout the martial arts community, and different types of training routines were often employed to strengthen them simultaneously. Some schools focused on practicing special breathing exercises. These exercises taught students how to breathe properly while also promoting a strong sense of balance.

Other schools practiced special balancing exercises using special pieces of equipment such as balance beams, posts, and bricks. By concentrating on developing physical balance, students unwittingly learned how to breathe properly! Many contemporary martial arts schools, such as yiliquan, xingyiquan, Okinawan Goju-ryu, and Uechi-ryu, feature training with both breathing exercises and a number of special balancing or footwork drills. Although proper breathing is heavily emphasized during the practice of basic techniques and fighting drills, it is also unconsciously trained through the practice of special footwork and body-shifting exercises.

Breathing Through the Feet

The late Master W. C. Chen would often have me practice standing on bricks as I practiced my solo postures. When I first began this routine, I would weave back and forth, shake, and sometimes flail my arms about as I struggled to maintain my balance. Chen would chuckle and just say, "Breathe! You have to breathe!"

Of course I have to breathe! I don't need to be reminded about that! It's my balance that's the problem.

Chen let me struggle through a couple of sessions before he came up to me and pointed to my feet. "Breathe from *there!* Then you can balance." Noticing the look of utter confusion on my face, he explained further. "Breathe through the bottoms of your feet and put your mind at your dantien so you won't be so afraid," he said. "Your breathing is too high and you are frightened. That is the problem."

I took his advice and began to imagine that I was breathing through the yongquan points on the soles of my feet. I found that the deep abdominal breathing helped me to relax and, within a few seconds, I had calmed down considerably. I experienced much less difficulty in maintaining my balance on those bricks from that day on. I had learned a most valuable lesson, indeed!

Chapter 11

The Importance of Spinal Alignment

Stand Up Straight!

In order to unify your upper and lower body so that you can move powerfully from your dantien you must maintain proper alignment of the spinal column. This sounds easy enough to do, but it actually requires considerable practice. It's a skill that requires constant cultivation, so if you restrict your practice of spinal symmetry only to the time you spend in the training hall, it will never become an unconscious habit.

"Why does it have to become an unconscious habit?" you ask. Because when the chips are down and you're up against an opponent who's built and looks like a professional hockey player, when the pucker factor goes through the ceiling and adrenaline is being pumped into your system by the gallon, you have neither the time nor the inclination to stop and think about whether your spine is correctly aligned. So, start practicing *now* to make it a natural aspect of your posture.

Press the Head Upward

Stiffening your back or neck will deadlock your energy and cause you to move with all the agility and grace of a wooden soldier. Spinal

Figure 11-1

alignment must be managed without excessively tensing the muscles of your back or neck. To accomplish this you'll begin by gently raising the crown of the head.

The Taijiquan Classics remind us to "press the head upward" or to "hold the head as if suspended by a string (from above)." Personally, I find it easier to do if I imagine trying to touch my head to a low ceiling that is only an inch or so above my head. By "pushing the crown upward" the cervical vertebrae are "pushed" straight and aligned with the thoracic vertebrae (Figure 11-1).

Common Errors

- *Don't arch your neck backward and lift your chin or tighten your jaw.* There shouldn't be any tension in this subtle adjustment of your cervical vertebrae.
- *Be careful that you don't try to "hide your ears" with your shoulders.* Keep your shoulders dropped and relaxed.

Tuck the Coccyx

The coccyx should be tucked slightly in and upward, directed toward your dantien (Figure 11-2). This helps keep the thoracic vertebrae straight and aligned with the cervical vertebrae. It gently "stretches" the lower part of the spinal column and creates a kind of compression within the dantien, which will enable you to emit considerable power.

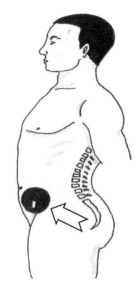

Figure 11-2

If this alignment is maintained throughout the execution of a body movement or technique, the structural integrity of the body will be secure.

Common Errors

Unless you're in training to become an exotic dancer, *don't push your coccyx too far forward and "flatten" your lower back.* This inordinate movement will only serve to diminish your power.

Spinal Alignment and Kicking

Although maintaining proper spinal alignment is relatively easy to do when you're performing upper-body techniques, kicking techniques are another story.

Lower-body techniques such as the side thrust kick, back thrust kick, and roundhouse kick require you to lean slightly, so a subsequent loss of power is unavoidable. However, practicing various stretching exercises to increase your flexibility will help diminish the degree to which you must lean and, consequently, the amount of power you lose. That's right! If you want strong kicks you need to s-t-r-e-t-c-h! Regularly.

Testing the Effectiveness of Spinal Alignment

So, you think all this spinal alignment stuff is so much twaddle, huh? Well, let's try four little tests.

Figure 11-3

■ Test One

Stand in a stable stance and extend one fist as if punching. Have a partner grasp your wrist and attempt to pull you off-balance (Figure 11-3).

If your spine is properly aligned, your posture will be quite stable. However, if you lean in any direction, your partner will be able to pull you forward without much difficulty (Figures 11-4 and 11-5).

Figure 11-4

Figure 11-5

■ Test Two

Begin as in Test One. As your partner tries to pull you off-balance, bow your head forward or tilt it backward (Figures 11-6 and 11-7). You will find that he is easily able to move you. Keeping your cervical vertebrae straight and pushing the crown upward are crucial to maintaining a stable posture from which you can issue power.

Figure 11-6

Figure 11-7

■ Test Three

Have your partner stand normally with one arm extended. As you grasp his wrist and attempt to pull him toward you, bend your back or neck in any direction (Figures 11-8 and 11-9). You will find that you are unable to move him. Your strength is significantly reduced.

Figure 11-8

Figure 11-9

Figure 11-10

However, if you maintain correct spinal alignment, you will be able to pull him off-balance without too much difficulty (Figure 11-10).

■ Test Four

Try this test to measure your stability in kicking.

   Stand in front of your partner. Bring your knee up as if to execute a kick. As you do so, your partner should push down on the
top of your knee in an attempt to force your leg back down. If you
are maintaining correct vertebral alignment, he will be unable to
do so (Figures 11-11 and 11-12).

Figure 11-11

Figure 11-12

Additional Benefits

Do you slump when you're sitting? Yeah, I saw you suddenly straighten
up. So, do you walk or stand with a slouch, too? People stand and sit
in slumped positions because they're trying to relax. The problem is
that a slumped position is never comfortable for very long and you
have to change positions rather frequently.

Being relaxed isn't the same as being flaccid. When your body sags like a bag of soggy rice, the internal viscera are scrunched together and the weight of the body isn't distributed properly. If you need to move quickly and suddenly, you're out of luck (Figures 11-13 and 11-14).

Figure 11-13

Figure 11-14

On the other hand, if you push your head up away from your shoulders when you stand up or sit down, your posture will be restful and your organs will be held in their proper positions (Figures 11-15 and 11-16). This actually has an additional positive impact on your overall health.

 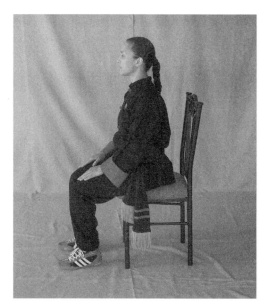

Figure 11-15   **Figure 11-16**

People who are always slouched are often rather unhealthy. They catch colds easily and, whenever a new strain of flu comes around, they nearly always succumb to it. Their immune systems are weak because their crumpled postures interfere with the free flow of qi through the body's energy pathways.

Chapter 12

Don't Isolate...Consolidate!

All Persons Are Created Equal

If ten people perform a basic punch and they all do it differently, there are only two possibilities:

They're all doing it wrong, or

One person is doing it correctly and everyone else is doing it wrong.

Why can't they all be doing it right? Well, what if you asked them to add 2 plus 2 and each person came up with a different answer? The same two possibilities would apply. So long as each person gives a different answer, they can't all be right. Right?

Because all human beings possess basically the same musculature, skeletal structure, and nervous systems, and because we are all subject to the same unalterable laws of physics, there can be only one most efficient way of performing a reverse punch or any other technique. So, if you want to maximize the strength and efficiency of any given type of physical movement, it behooves you to examine how you can best utilize the strength and structure of your body and the principles by which it works. In this chapter we'll examine several basic principles that can make significant differences in the efficiency of your techniques.

Figure 12-1

Figure 12-2

Figure 12-3

Principles of Upper-Body Techniques

The Secret Chamber

Some forms of karate and kung-fu chamber the punching fist at the level of the nipple, while others favor a chamber at the center of the chest, or just above the edge of the pelvis on the iliac crest (Figures 12-1 to 12-3).

Many schools regard these disparities as nothing more than stylistic differences and insist that the positioning of the fist prior to the execution of the punch really has little to do with the amount of power one is able to generate. They are wrong.

I'll bet that statement won't make me a lot of new friends, but it's true. Just consider what happens if the punching fist is initially chambered at the level of the nipple or upper chest:

- Because the punching elbow is placed *below* the level of the fist and the shoulder is slightly raised, the pectoral muscle is isolated. This restricts the punch to using only the strength of the single pectoral muscle rather than the larger and stronger abdominal muscles.
- The internal schools of kung-fu tell us that the shoulder should "push through" the elbow and the elbow should subsequently "push through" the fist (Figures 12-4 and 12-5). Failure to do this will result in a significant reduction of striking power.

Figure 12-4   **Figure 12-5**

Because the elbow is held on a plane lower than the fist, the force of the thrust cannot travel from the shoulder through the elbow and the elbow is unable to push through the fist. Instead, the power bypasses the elbow and travels directly from the shoulder to the fist, resulting in a loss of striking power.

Chambering the fist at the hip or at the level of the waist places the elbow on a plane *above* the fist. This allows the shoulder to push through the elbow and the elbow to push through the fist. The pectoral muscles are not isolated and more of the body's mass can be brought into play, thereby increasing the power of the thrust.

Dropping the Elbow

The traditional teachings of the internal schools constantly admonish us to keep the elbows "hanging down" as much as possible when delivering a blow. The reason for this is clear: Allowing the elbow to turn outward isolates the pectoral muscle, and severely curtails the strength of the technique. Try two simple tests.

■ Test One

Stand in a stable stance and extend one arm as if you are executing a corkscrew punch. Place it against the chest of your partner and allow the elbow to point out to the side (Figure 12-6). Have your partner lean his weight against your arm as you try to resist his force.

Your arm will collapse shortly after he begins to exert force (Figure 12-7). This is because you are restricted to using the isolated strength of your pectoral muscle to resist the weight of his whole body.

Figure 12-6

Figure 12-7

■ Test Two

Now "roll" your elbow downward and try to resist your partner again (Figure 12-8). You will feel most of his power being dissipated out through the sole of your rear foot, and your arm will not collapse. This is because your pectoral muscle is no longer isolated and you are able to utilize the strength of your whole body.

The bengquan thrust of xingyiquan automatically drops the elbow straight down, eliminating the possibility of pectoral isolation (Figure 12-9).

Figure 12-8

Figure 12-9

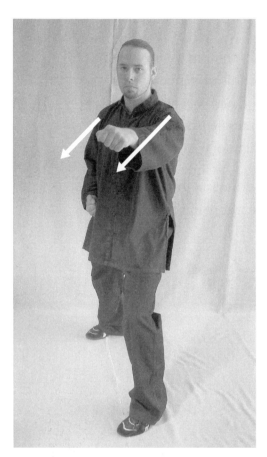

Figure 12-10

Staying Inside the Lines

Imagine two lines extending straight out from your shoulders (Figure 12-10).

All of your frontal upper-body techniques should be performed so that your elbows and hands remain inside these parallel lines. The farther your elbows or hands extend beyond these lines, the weaker they become. If your elbows jut out beyond these "shoulder lines," you will not be able to strike or perform any upper-body technique with full body power.

Don't think so, huh? You think I'm just being persnickety? Try two more tests.

■ Test Three

Stand in a forward stance and extend one fist as if executing a punch, but punch outside the shoulder line. Try to resist your partner as he leans his full body weight against the front of your fist. You'll find that you are unable to do so. This is because his force cannot be directed straight down your arm and into the sole of your rear foot (Figure 12-11).

Now execute a high block with your elbow extended outside of the shoulder line (Figure 12-12). Try to resist your partner as he pulls down on your forearm. Your arm will collapse easily (Figure 12-13).

Figure 12-11

Figure 12-12

Figure 12-13

■ Test Four

Repeat Test Three above, but be sure to keep your hand and elbow inside the shoulder line. You will be able to easily resist your partner's force (Figures 12-14 and 12-15).

Figure 12-14

Figure 12-15

"Ten-Hut!"

A line of soldiers snapping to attention looks sharp and square, but performing martial arts techniques with this kind of box-like positioning only results in separation of the upper and lower body, isolation of certain muscle groups, and a subsequent loss of stability and power.

The human body doesn't contain sharp angles like a rectangle. It's composed of gentle curves. Bending any joint to an angle of 90 degrees or more significantly reduces its ability to generate or resist force.

For instance, if you extend your arm and keep the elbow slightly flexed you will be able to push forcefully and easily resist the reaction force you generate (Figure 12-16).

However, if the arm is bent at 90 degrees or more, your ability to generate force is considerably reduced (Figure 12-17).

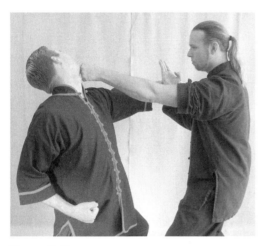 

Figure 12-16   **Figure 12-17**

Ancient texts and "songs" left to us by past masters of the martial arts enjoin us to drop the shoulders. They shouldn't be pushed down forcefully. They're simply relaxed. The chest should be slightly concave. In this way power can easily be generated from the abdominal muscles, which are the strongest muscles in the body. Conversely, if the chest is arched out or the shoulders are raised or pulled back (as when standing in the military posture of *attention*), the muscles of the chest are isolated and the tremendous strength of the abdominal muscles cannot be utilized. Arching the chest or raising the shoulders also stretches the diaphragm upward, preventing you from being able to utilize reverse breathing (see Chapter 10).

Principles of Lower-Body Techniques
Driving the Kick

When you perform a front kick, with which foot do you actually kick? Is it the foot that hits the target or your supporting foot?

If your technique is correct, you should really be kicking with your supporting foot because it's the one that's driving against the ground and moving your hips into the kick! This is the foot that provides the real power for your technique. On the other hand (or foot), if you're simply standing on your supporting foot—balancing on it instead of driving it against the ground—you cannot utilize the integrated power of your whole body when you deliver your kick. You're merely swatting your opponent with the isolated power of your kicking leg (Figures 12-18 and 12-19).

Figure 12-18

Figure 12-19

Learning to drive your supporting foot against the ground when you kick isn't easy. It has to be initiated at the very beginning of your kick, just before the kicking foot leaves the ground. It requires a good deal of practice to get the feel of it.

Kicking Out and Returning along the Same Plane

In kicks that utilize a knee snap, be sure that the kicking foot begins and ends in exactly the same position. Remember how you used to wind up your towel and snap your buddies on the butt in the locker room? It's the same thing. If you didn't quickly whip your towel out and back along the same plane, what happened? Nothing, except that your intended victim probably punched you in the mouth while you were still whistling the theme to "Rawhide." But if your towel snapped out and back along the same plane, you could get a nice whipping effect and maybe leave a decent welt on your victim's backside, right?

The same principle applies to kicks that utilize a knee snap—the front snap kick, front thrust kick, side thrust kick, roundhouse kick, and back thrust kick. Bear in mind that snap kicks such as the front snap kick and roundhouse kick whip out and back quickly and follow an arc. Thrust kicks such as the back thrust kick, front thrust kick, and side thrust kick travel out and back in a straight line. They don't snap back with the same celerity as the snap kicks because they are intended to produce a different type of impact.

Figure 12-20

Don't Push . . . Kick!

If you're too close to your opponent when you deliver your kick, the knee of your kicking leg will be substantially bent. This means that you're going to deliver a hearty push rather than a sharp kick (Figure 12-20).

Actually, you'll probably push yourself off-balance since you're standing on only one foot.

Your kicking foot should hit the target with no more than about 2 inches of extension left in the leg. This ensures that you'll deliver maximum power with your kick (Figure 12-21).

Figure 12-21

"Hold It Right There!"

In the Chinese martial arts there is a principle that states that the height at which you can elevate and hold your foot is the height to which you can effectively kick. Kicking above this height requires that you rely exclusively on momentum, which means that you don't have complete control over your kick.

You think your kicks are pretty spiffy? Try this exercise.

■ Exercise: Holding the Kick Height

Hold your leg out in a front kick or side kick position for 40 seconds. Bring it back to the chambered position for 5 seconds, and then extend it out again (Figures 12-22 through 12-24). Do this three times.

Could you do it? Did you have a religious experience and see God? Practice stretching and try to gradually increase the height of your kick and the length of time you can hold it.

Figure 12-22   **Figure 12-23**   **Figure 12-24**

Chapter 13

The Fighting Stance

Overcoming Inertia

Newton's First Law of Motion states:

> *An object in motion or at rest tends to remain in motion or at rest and*
> *at the same rate of speed and in the same direction unless acted upon*
> *by some external force.*

This resistance to change is known as *inertia*.

So, what does this have to do with your martial arts training?
Plenty.

When you're about to go full-tilt boogie with someone who means
to rearrange your facial structure, you have to overcome your body's
natural resistance to the changes you're about to make in the velocity and direction of your movement. If you try to overcome your
body's inertia by applying brute force or by using the isolated movements of an arm, a leg, or a foot, the resulting movement will be disjointed and weak. The end result can be embarrassing as well as very
painful.

In combat, transitions in movement must be made smoothly and
quickly. You've got to get your body to work with you instead of
against you. This can be accomplished if you begin your movements
from a stable but highly mobile and "loaded" fighting stance.

What Is a Fighting Stance?

A *fighting stance* can best be defined as a posturing of the body, mind, and spirit in preparation for combat. No single stance is better than any other, although there are certainly some that are worse than others. Consider the requirements of an effective fighting stance:

- It must be stable
- It must be highly mobile in all directions
- It must bring as many of your (bodily) weapons up front as possible

Some martial arts enthusiasts fight from a cat stance (Figure 13-1). This stance is very mobile and brings three of the body's four main weapons—both hands and both feet—to the fore. The front foot can be used to kick very quickly and both hands are up front and available for immediate use. It sure looks efficient … but it's not stable at all. About 90 percent of the body's weight is on the rear foot, which means that the front foot lacks a firm root.

Figure 13-1   **Figure 13-2**   **Figure 13-3**

Another popular fighting posture is the horse-riding stance (Figure 13-2). This wide stance is very stable to the sides. Unfortunately, it's not very mobile at all and the only bodily weapon that is available for immediate use is the leading hand. To use the rear hand or either foot requires a major body shift that is readily apparent to your opponent—and it's never a good idea to let your enemy know what you're about to do.

Select a stance that is comfortable for you. It mustn't be so wide that mobility is lost nor should it be so narrow that it is unstable. Figure 13-3 shows a fighting position that is very stable, highly mobile, and spring-loaded.

Standing on a Hair Trigger

Never stand "dead" in your fighting stance. A "dead stance" is one that lacks potential energy. You just sit in it like a duck floating on the calm water of a pond.

And like a duck, you're a very easy, accessible target.

In combat, things happen very quickly and unexpectedly. When you need to move, you must be able to overcome your body's natural resistance to movement and act instantly. A proper fighting stance allows you to do this. It should be spring-loaded, as if your posture is set on a hair trigger. Here's how to "load" your stance:

- Contract the muscles of the inner thighs very *slightly*
- Contract the anal sphincter *slightly*
- Grip the ground *slightly* with the toes

Moving in a Fighting Stance

Let's get one thing straight right away: I don't approve of bouncing around on the balls of the feet. "But that's what boxers do," you say. Fine, but bear in mind that first and foremost, boxing is a sport! In a boxing match the contestants are required to wear padded gloves. They're not allowed to kick, or strike with their elbows. If they manage to knock the opponent down, they're required to step back and allow him to get back on his feet. Remember that in a real fight there are no roped-off rings, no gloves, no groin cups, and no referees. There are no rules and no trophies for second place.

When you bounce around, your center of gravity is never stable. It's constantly moving up and down. When you're on your toes, you have absolutely no stability at all. If your opponent's timing is sharp, he can take advantage of this moment of vulnerability and attack when your center of gravity is rising. Because you lack a solid platform from which you can launch your defensive maneuvers and techniques, you're helpless and unable to defend yourself. There is a technical martial arts term that aptly describes people whose opponents catch them in such an untenable condition. It is *dogmeat*.

Never move just to be moving. In actual combat you move only when you must, or when it is to your advantage. Your shifting steps should be rather small. Avoid lifting your stepping foot as you would when you're taking a stroll, lest you expose yourself to sudden foot sweeps.

If your stance is properly loaded, you can advance by relaxing the muscles of the inner thighs and pressing your rear foot against the ground as your front foot advances. The rear foot is then brought forward and the adductors contract again to reload your stance (Figures 13-4 and 13-5). Above all, move from your dantien!

Figure 13-4

Figure 13-5

When you step backward, simply press your front foot against the ground as your rear foot retreats. The front foot is then squeezed back and the stance is instantly reloaded (Figures 13-6 and 13-7).

Figure 13-6

Figure 13-7

In moving laterally, press the driving foot against the ground as you step to the side with the other foot. The driving foot is then immediately brought over in a squeezing action (Figures 13-8 to 13-11).

Figure 13-8

Figure 13-9

Figure 13-10

Figure 13-11

Positioning the Upper Body

First off, don't bring your fists up as if you're boxing (Figure 13-12). Remember that boxers aren't allowed to kick. Bad guys can and do. If you hold both hands up in a boxer's stance, you'll be unable to effectively deflect attacks to your legs and groin.

Avoid front-facing your opponent (Figure 13-13). This exposes too much of your upper body to sudden attack and if you fire a quick punch, you won't be able to properly rotate your waist into it.

Side-facing the opponent isn't much better (Figure 13-14). It may make you a smaller target, but to strike the opponent requires you to make a large and obvious body shift.

The preferred position for the upper body is half-front facing (Figure 13-15). The upper body is turned inward up to 45 degrees. This position doesn't expose too much of your upper body and it permits quick rotation of the waist.

Figure 13-12

Figure 13-13

Figure 13-14

Figure 13-15

Fast versus Sudden

It's one thing to develop lightning-fast punches and kicks, but it's something else to be able to close the distance between yourself and your foe and deliver your techniques effectively. You must learn to move abruptly and quickly without inadvertently "telegraphing" your intentions to your opponent. This kind of sudden, explosive movement can be effected only if you begin from a stable, "loaded" posture.

An excellent way to practice is to stand in front of a full-length mirror. As you face your image, look for and eliminate subtle, telltale signals such as the shifting of a foot, dipping a shoulder, tightening your jaw, raising your eyebrows, pursing your lips, and so on. The list is almost endless. When you can step and strike without any tip-offs, you've got it.

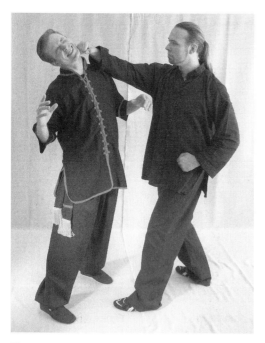

Figure 13-16

Fighting Stances in the Real World

Self-defense situations in the real world rarely involve two combatants "putting up their dukes" and squaring off against each other. Usually, the aggressor will initiate his attack when you're standing in a relatively neutral posture (Figure 13-16). He may begin with a push, which is actually intended to set you up for his best sucker punch. He may attempt a grab, or he may skip the foreplay and just unload on you all at once.

You never know what's going to happen when an antagonist behaves in a threatening manner. You have to expect the unexpected—be ready for anything. When a potentially hostile scumbag confronts you, you don't want to provoke or threaten him. At the same time, you have to be prepared to take control of the situation if things go south. In Figure 13-17 our model has placed one foot slightly ahead of the other. This helps ensure good balance and allows movement quickly in any direction. The adductors should be slightly tensed to "load" the stance so that you can move very quickly if the need arises. The anal sphincter should be slightly contracted as you prepare to move from your dantien at a moment's notice.

If the conflict is preceded by an argument or a threat, you may raise your hands in what appears to be a defensive gesture (like the model, as he tells the hothead to calm down, in Figure 13-18). Notice that one hand is placed ahead of the other. Although this gesture

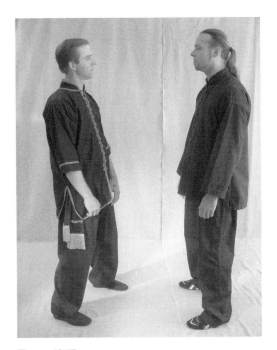

Figure 13-17

Figure 13-18

appears harmless, its real intention is to bring the hands up so that they can be quickly employed defensively or offensively.

It's a good idea to practice both defensive and offensive maneuvers from these "natural stances."

Chapter 14

The Mechanic's Shop

Putting It All Together

You say you're confused and you can't figure out how to put all of this stuff together? Well, kick away the footrest, get on your feet, and follow these simple instructions. We'll move from the bottom up. Literally.

Starting from the Feet and Ankles

The feet should feel as though the yongquan points are "suctioned" to the ground (Figure 14-1), like those little suction cups on the paws of the stuffed cat that you stick in the back window of your car. This means that the toes have to grip the ground like little claws. Get a grip, but don't clamp down so hard that the tension goes up to your knees. If you concentrate on "embracing the ground" with your big and pinkie toes, the others will follow suit.

Don't tense your ankles. Just grip the ground firmly with your feet and shove your driving foot *through* the ground. This applies not only to upper-body techniques but to kicking techniques, too. Once your technique hits the target, you'll be able to generate a secondary reaction force (shock).

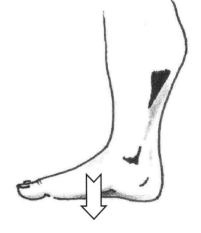

Figure 14-1

The weight of your body mustn't sit on your heels or on the balls of your feet, lest you lose your balance when the reaction force of your blow zips back through your body and down to your driving foot. Your weight has to be settled into the centers of the soles of your feet.

The angle at which the driving foot pushes into the ground is also important. If the angle is wrong, you'll lose power. To determine if the angle of your drive is correct and whether your stance is stable, practice standing on squares of cardboard as you drive your rear foot into the ground and execute a powerful thrust. If you suddenly find yourself lying on the floor wondering who you are, you need more work.

Up through the Legs

Thrusting your driving foot downward while simultaneously gripping the ground with your toes will automatically bring the larger

muscles of the legs into play. In fact, the driving foot must not only press into the ground; it must *feel as though it is screwing into* the ground. The key word here is *feel*. Although they don't actually rotate, the driving foot and leg should feel as though they are being screwed into the earth (Figure 14-2).

Although the knee of the rear (driving) leg will feel the screwing effect of the rear (driving) foot, make sure that you don't straighten it! Remember, once it's completely straightened and the knee is locked, you can't thrust your foot

Figure 14-2

against the ground, and you will be unable to transmit power from your driving foot. The knee of your forward leg must not wobble as you perform your technique. If it does, your root will be broken and your posture will be destabilized.

Now, if you're pressing and screwing the driving foot into the ground, you'll notice that the buttock on that side tenses slightly inward. That's fine. Actually, you should slightly tense both buttocks inward as if you're trying to hold a grape between your buttocks. To get the full effect of this tension in the buttocks, you must also tighten the anal sphincter somewhat and tuck the coccyx in and upward. Direct the tip of your coccyx up toward your dantien. It is this seemingly irrelevant but absolutely crucial movement that really helps unite the muscle connections and strength of the upper and lower body. It acts as a sort of "sacral pump" to draw qi up through the soles of the feet, through the legs, round the waist, and up the spine.

To the Hips and Waist

The *gua*—the area of hips, lower back, and abdominal muscles— plays a major role in the execution of effective technique. Chinese martial arts teachers refer to this large area as the "waist," while Japanese and Okinawan karate instructors dub it the "hips." Both disciplines are actually alluding to the same large area of the body, which consists of several parts.

The gua (also spelled *kua*) is actually the inguinal crease. It is a very important part of the body core (especially in the practice of internal forms of kung-fu) because if it isn't manipulated correctly, your ability to effectively emit internal power will be seriously hampered. It consists largely of the iliopsoas muscle (Figure 14-3).

When you sit properly in a horse-riding stance, you should sit straight down from the gua. A simple way to do this is to spread your feet to the proper width and then place your hands on your hips so that your forefingers point down into the inguinal crease. As you press straight down, your hips will sink and you will sit into the gua correctly. When you sit in the gua it is "closed." This same method of sitting in the gua is performed in the other main stances as well.

When you execute a hand strike, the gua on the side of the striking hand must be pushed forward (which causes it to "open") while the gua on the other side is pulled back and "closed." This is easiest to do with techniques that involve the body action of rotation (see Chapter 8).

The area of the acupuncture point known as *ming-men* (located in the lumbar area) must expand slightly (Figure 14-4). I liken this feeling to that of a tortoise sunning its back on a rock.

The abdominal muscles come into play through the application of reverse breathing (see Chapter 9). These are the strongest muscles in the body and they absolutely must be used whenever you execute an upper- or lower-body technique.

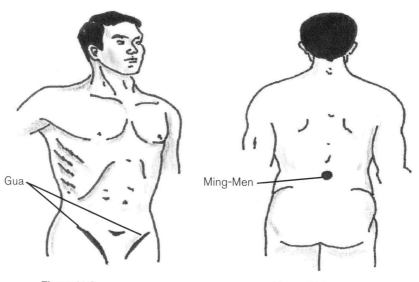

Figure 14-3   **Figure 14-4**

Up the Spine and Out through the Hands

In Chapter 11, you were shown why it's important to align the lumbar, thoracic, and cervical vertebrae, and in Chapter 12, I talked about the importance of dropping the shoulders, hanging the elbows, and "swallowing" the chest. Here's where it all comes home to roost. As the power is driven up through your legs and waist, it now moves up the spine.

Common Errors

■ *If your spine is bent, the power is unable to travel smoothly up and over your shoulders and you'll be unable to strike with your full potential* (Figure 14-5). This is equally true of kicking techniques (Figure 14-6).

Figure 14-5

Figure 14-6

- *If your shoulders are raised, tensed, or "squared," the power stops at your chest.* It's choked off from being able to travel down your arm to your hand (Figure 14-7).
- *If the elbow of your striking hand is held out to the side, the majority of the reaction force of your blow will pass through it and dissipate into space* (Figure 14-8).
- *Do not tense your hand!* If the striking surface is properly aligned with your wrist, elbow, and shoulder, the impact of your blow will create the required tension for you! Deliberately tensing your hand cuts the power off at your wrist.

So, there. Don't hurry. If you try to be attentive to all of these fine points of total body integration while firing off multiple techniques at full throttle, you'll never get it right. You have to take it step by step. Practice slowly and get the feel of it as you build speed and power incrementally.

Figure 14-7

Figure 14-8

Chapter 15

Techniques in Combination

What Is a Combination?

A combination consists of two or more techniques that are executed in rapid succession. You say that you already knew that? Let's find out how much you really know about your combinations, okay? Stand up and fire off your best combo and then we'll take a little quiz.

Go ahead. Don't skip ahead and see what's next. That's cheating. Get out of your recliner and do it!

Done? Great! Here's a short quiz. Answer these questions honestly:

How many techniques were involved in your combination?

How much distance did you cover?

How long did it take for you to complete your combination?

Did you lose your balance at any time?

How many breaths did you use?

Now let's look at some hard facts about combinations and see if your answers match up.

Why a Combination?

So, what is the reason for executing a combination? Bear in mind that we're not talking about scoring points here. We're talking about real self-defense, where mistakes such as a loss of balance or a slight hesitation can be very expensive. If your mistakes are really bad, you may inadvertently help put your surgeon's son through college.

The function of a combination is very simple: It's used to fire a powerful barrage of techniques into the enemy while you *take his ground*. Never throw a combination with the intention of simply holding your ground. The objective in any fight is to penetrate through the opponent, take his piece of real estate, and crush him! You must endeavor to keep the enemy on the defensive. As long as he's in a defensive mode, his ability to strike back at you is severely impaired. However, if you fail to hurt him or if you halt your aggressive momentum, your opponent can quickly recover and take the offensive, thereby effectively reversing roles. Don't give him a chance to recover. Drive through him and bring him down as quickly as possible.

Here endeth the lesson.

Finding Combinations That Work

In order for a combination to be effective, the techniques and body actions involved in its execution must flow into each other as smoothly as possible. Figures 15-1 to 15-4 show a very basic and smooth combination that consists of a jab, a reverse punch, and a kick. You needn't adjust your position as you move from one technique to the next. The end of one technique is literally the beginning of the next. You are continuously moving into the enemy and there are no pauses between techniques.

Figure 15-1

Figure 15-2

Figure 15-3

Figure 15-4

Figure 15-5

Figure 15-6

Figure 15-7

Figures 15-5 to 15-7 depict a combination of techniques that don't blend very well: a reverse punch, followed by a kick with the front leg, and then a rear-leg kick. Why is this combination likely to fail?

Think about it. There are a couple of major flaws here:

- The first and most obvious flaw is that in order to execute the kick with his front leg, our model must momentarily halt his advance and shift his weight to the rear. His forward momentum is stalled and there will be a distinct pause between his jab and the front-leg kick. This creates an opening—a break in our model's flow of movement that a skilled opponent can readily exploit.

- This same kind of pause will occur between the two kicks. Unless our boy has been secretly learning how to levitate, he will have to place his front foot back on the ground before executing the second kick.

- The front-leg kick also prevents advancing forward and taking ground. This allows the enemy to safely retreat and recover.

I can see the guy in the back waving his hand and shouting, "But how about using multiple kicks with the same foot? That's a really effective combination! I've used it many times and I always won!"

Yeah, sure. Won what? A point? Try that kind

of silliness on the street and your opponent may very well unscrew your leg and shove it ... well, somewhere. Two kicks delivered with the same foot may work (see Figures 15-8 to 15-10). But more than two?

Nope, not a chance.

Why? Because after you deliver your first kick your supporting foot can't drive against the ground. That means that you're restricted to using the isolated power of your elevated leg. You can execute a second kick at the enemy's knee if you really torque your hips into it, but if you try to kick above the level of your own waist you're not going to generate much power.

Figure 15-8

After the second kick has been completed, you're out of gas. Your momentum is pretty much spent and your kicks won't have much gusto at all. If your opponent hasn't already done so, he'll probably grab your leg and turn you into a human posthole digger.

Figure 15-9

It's important to remember that real fights don't happen like they do in front of a motion picture camera. Even if they're accomplished martial arts practitioners, actors have to make large, overt movements that will leave their fans all a-twitter. In reality, any streetwise thug would easily counter such obvious movements. The most effective fighting techniques are much more subtle and, frankly, a lot more brutal. An experienced fighter lets the opponent's movements determine just what he's going to do.

Figure 15-10

Quality versus Quantity

Many years ago, when I was only a fledgling student under the revered kung-fu master, W. C. Chen, one of my older classmates approached me and tried to intimidate me by demonstrating how many strikes he could deliver in the span of one second. "I can strike you at least five times in a second," Lum boasted. Then, bringing his hands up in an on-guard position, he fired off a number of blindingly fast punches and strikes, pulling all of them just short of contact with my face. Unfortunately, he hadn't noticed that our teacher had walked up behind him.

"Huh," Chen grumped. Lum froze and his jaw dropped as he turned around. "I am not so fast," Chen said quietly. "I can only hit him once. But I only need to hit him once."

Chen smiled as he turned and walked away. Lum never bragged about his machine-gun strikes again.

Combinations and Breathing

Correct breathing plays an essential role in the development of powerful, effective combinations. It's one thing to breathe properly when you deliver a single technique, but learning to breathe correctly when you deliver multiple techniques is another matter altogether. It's going to require a good deal of practice, so put down your bowl of nachos and pay attention.

A complete breath consists of four parts:

An inhalation

A brief pause

An exhalation

Another pause

There are two pauses in each and every breath. The pause that occurs at the end of an exhalation (but before the next inhalation) is usually the longer of the two. Remember what I said in Chapter 10 about being vulnerable when the breath is being inhaled or when it's paused? If you don't, you have a serious reading retention problem. You'll notice that three of the four parts of a complete breath leave you vulnerable. When you inhale or pause your breath:

Your body's ability to resist a blow is considerably decreased

Your reaction time is increased

Your speed is reduced

Remember how many techniques you fired in the combination you executed at the beginning of this chapter? Did you breathe out with each one? If you did, you botched it.

Why? Because if you exhaled with each technique you did one of two things, both of which are taboo:

You either inhaled between your techniques, or

You held your breath between your techniques, creating a distinct pause at the conclusion of each technique

And what happens when you inhale or pause your breath? An opponent whose timing is sharp can easily capitalize on these moments of vulnerability and unload a devastating attack. So, what can you do to prevent this from happening? The answer is obvious: *Fire your entire combination in the space of a single exhalation!* If you can't do it, you either have too many techniques in your combination or you need to work on increasing your lung capacity.

Don't cheat and increase the length of your breath. Remember that the faster you exhale, the faster you move. Exhale your breath as quickly as possible and fit your techniques into that small amount of time. And don't forget to use reverse breathing! Performing two techniques in one exhalation isn't too difficult to do, but launching three or more strong techniques will take some considerable practice.

Chapter 16

Comedy, Love, and Martial Arts

Borrowing the Opponent's Force

Yeah, I know that the name of this chapter is a little confusing. But think about it. What do comedy, love, and martial arts have in common?

Timing!

Timing is that wonderful principle that enables you to do what your boss expects of you every day—it is how to do more with less.

Using Timing to Your Advantage

If an object is moving forward with a force of 100 pounds and another object strikes it head-on with 50 pounds of force, how much force is involved in the collision?

If you guessed that the answer is 150 pounds, you're right. So, if your opponent is moving toward you with, say, 150 pounds of force and you drive into him with 100 pounds of force, there's a total of about 250 pounds of force involved. The force with which he is advancing is added to the force of your blow (Figure 16-1).

No, the opponent doesn't necessarily absorb all of it. Whoever is the least stable will absorb most of it. That's one reason why you have to practice regularly to sharpen your body movements and tech-

Figure 16-1

niques as much as possible. And you have to hone your timing to a razor's edge so that you are able to catch the opponent at the instant he's the most vulnerable—in the middle of his movement.

Your posture, from the end of your striking foot or fist to the sole of your driving foot, must be perfectly aligned so that it is capable of withstanding the full amount of force involved in this scenario. Any weakness in your posture will be magnified with the return of the reaction force. For instance, if you're leaning backward your stance is unstable, and you may end up pushing yourself away from the opponent (Figure 16-2).

If your punching wrist or kicking ankle is weak or misaligned (or both), the reaction force may cause the joint to buckle, resulting in a nasty injury. But if your posture is stable and correctly aligned, most (but not all) of the reaction force will rebound, traveling up from the sole of your driving foot to the point of impact where it will be returned to the opponent. He will be struck with his advancing force as well as yours.

Figure 16-2

Figure 16-3

On the other hand, if he's moving away from your blow at the instant of impact, the force with which he's moving is subtracted from the force of your blow. So, if you strike with a force of 100 pounds and he's back-pedaling with a force of 50 pounds at the moment of impact, he will receive only 50 pounds of your force (Figure 16-3).

If the opponent is not moving at all at the instant of impact, his force is zero. The only force involved is yours.

The Advantages of Sharp Timing

A fighter who is able to move quickly and hit hard, with sharp timing, has some distinct advantages over an opponent who lacks these abilities.

- He is able to use the enemy's force against him.
- He can catch the opponent at just the right moment, when he is absolutely helpless and unable to adequately defend himself. This is especially true if the opponent is struck while initiating

an attack, when he is physically and mentally in an "attack mode" and unable to switch into a "defense mode" quickly enough to save his bacon.

- He doesn't need to strike with full power. If he can catch the opponent's attack in mid-stride, he can add the enemy's force to his own, thereby conserving his own energy.

Like everything else in martial arts, sharpening your timing will require a great deal of practice. It's not something you can achieve overnight; so don't try. Just take it one step at a time. You'll eventually get there.

What? Disadvantages?

You bet there are. Consider:

- If your timing is bad, you'll run straight into the enemy's blazing attack. You're punching yourself with the bad guy's fist.
- Let's say that your timing is great and you whack the opponent in mid-stride. You're close enough to swap spit with the guy but your technique has all the destructive power of a damp rag. There you are, having slugged your adversary with your strongest punch and he's just standing there, wondering if that's the best you've got. There is a common breakfast food that aptly describes what becomes of people who find themselves in this predicament. It is *toast*.

To make this whole timing thing work, you need more than sharp reflexes and quick movement. You need to be able to deliver powerful, effective technique!

Chapter 17

Horizontal Strength

'Tis Better to Give ...

When you execute a given technique, the object is to transfer as much of your striking power into the opponent as possible. One of the most effective ways to do this is to disrupt the enemy's balance and thereby render him incapable of resisting the energy of your blow. This is done through the application of what is known as *horizontal strength*.

The Third Foot

The so-called "third foot" is actually the opponent's center of gravity (CG). Why do I refer to it as a third foot?

Because it acts like one.

In Figure 17-1 our model is standing in a natural stance with his weight evenly distributed between both feet. The spot on the ground between his feet is actually where his body's center of gravity falls.

If you step onto this spot, your partner will feel slightly unbalanced (Figure 17-2). It's ... *unsettling*, both physically and psychologically. I don't know why this is true, but it is. Placing your foot on your

Figure 17-1

Figure 17-2

partner's CG causes a slight disruption in his mental and physical balance. Although this might seem like a rather insignificant oddity, it's something that can give you that little "extra edge."

Figures 17-3 to 17-5 show the CG of a forward stance, a back stance, and a horse-riding stance, respectively. You'll notice that the CG of a forward stance is not exactly centered between the feet; it's slightly forward of center. The CG of a back stance is slightly rear of center, and the CG of a horse-riding posture is centered midway between the feet.

If you step onto the CG of any of these stances, it will have the same effect as when your partner was standing in a natural position. If you drive powerfully onto the CG and stamp down on it as if you were executing a strong punch, the physical and mental disruption will be even more pronounced.

Whenever you penetrate into and through your enemy's posture, always seek to drive over his CG. Crush his third foot!

Figure 17-3

Figure 17-4

Figure 17-5

Displacing the Forward Stance

When I refer to a forward stance here, I'm actually referring to any stance that places the majority of the body's weight on the front foot (Figures 17-6 and 17-7).

Because the majority of the body's weight is carried on the front foot, this posture is highly resistant to frontal forces. If a force is received frontally, it is easily transmitted to the rear foot and the posture may remain quite stable (Figure 17-8).

Figure 17-6   **Figure 17-7**

Figure 17-8

Figure 17-9

The stance also has width, providing the opponent with some measure of resistance against lateral blows (Figure 17-9).

However, the stance is weak at the angles shown in Figure 17-10. Blows that penetrate the forward posture at these angles will completely destabilize the person.

Don't believe me? Try it for yourself, with the following exercise.

Figure 17-10

■ Exercise: Destabilizing the Forward Stance

Have your partner stand in a solid forward stance. If you push him from the front, he will easily resist your force (Figure 17-11).

Using very little strength, however, you can easily unbalance your partner by pushing through his stance at an angle (Figure 17-12).

Figure 17-11

Figure 17-12

Displacing the In-Line Stance

An in-line stance is any stance wherein the feet are aligned. This can include a horse-riding stance, cat stance, back stance, or even a forward stance that lacks width (Figures 17-13 to 17-16).

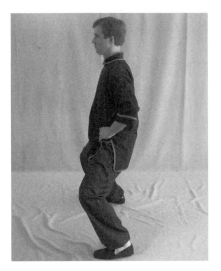

Figure 17-13

Figure 17-14

Figure 17-15

Figure 17-16

These stances are strong to the front and rear but they cannot resist blows that intersect their foundations from an angle or from the perpendicular (Figure 17-17).

Applying Horizontal Strength

Martial arts such as baguazhang, xingyiquan, and yiliquan specialize in the application of horizontal strength, moving out of the line of the opponent's attack and

Figure 17-17

striking from unexpected angles. These fighters generally do not oppose the enemy's force head-on. Rather, they employ evasive maneuvers that not only move them out of harm's way but that also place them in positions from which they can cut into the enemy's flanks.

Once you have succeeded in destabilizing the opponent's posture, you must press your attack, never giving the opponent the time or room to recover his balance. Penetrate your adversary's position, take his ground, and overwhelm him!

Chapter 18

Being Dense Is a Good Thing

The Importance of Density

Which item is most likely to cause damage if it hits you, a baseball bat or a Styrofoam cup?

Okay, that was an easy one. What if your choice was between a fist and an oak staff? If you answered that the staff would cause more damage, you're right. But why would it cause more damage than a human fist?

A twelve-year-old child isn't likely to hurt you too badly, even if he whacks you as hard as he can with his fist or foot. However, if you give the little sweetheart a knife or a hammer, he becomes down-right lethal. Why?

Part of the answer has to do with *density*.

What Is Density—And Why Does It Matter in Martial Arts?

There are two kinds of density: *weight density* and *mass density*. For our purposes we'll use mass density, which is mass per volume. Sound complicated? It isn't.

Lead is dense. Feathers are not. The metric system was designed so that water has a density of 1 gram per cubic centimeter (cc), or 1,000 grams per cubic meter.

Lead is ten times denser than water. It's also denser than Styrofoam or feathers, and, believe it or not, this is important stuff. Listen up.

If I hit you as hard as I can with a pound of poultry feathers, what will happen? You may swear off fried chicken for a month, but the blow certainly won't harm you. However, the result will be very different if I bash you in the forehead with a pound of lead. Why?

Differences in density.

Lead has greater density than feathers and because of that, there's a lot less "give" in a chunk of lead than there is in a bunch of feathers. Remember the concepts of initial force, reaction force, and shock (the secondary reaction force)? When the pound of feathers collides with your forehead, it is unable to withstand the force that is driving it forward. The pound of feathers collapses, absorbing almost 100 percent of the force into itself. Feathers are so flimsy that no significant initial impact is even generated. Knockouts are pretty rare in pillow-fights.

On the other hand, the pound of lead generates one heck of a wallop. It's solid and doesn't absorb much of its own force at all. Your forehead absorbs almost all of the force it generates.

So what does this have to do with martial arts?

Think about it.

One of the reasons the old-timers used to practice hitting a striking post or some similar device almost every day was to temper the striking surfaces of their hands. Among other things, this kind of training is intended to increase the density of the bones of the hands that are employed in various striking techniques. Hitting the striking post causes vibrations to travel through these bones, gradually increasing their density. When the striking surfaces become very dense they have less "give" in them and consequently, they'll absorb less of the force generated by the strike. This means that, in a fight, the opponent receives more of the striking force.

There is a popular misconception that this kind of training is intended to build heavy calluses on the striking surfaces of the hands. Certainly, the flesh will be toughened somewhat, but it needn't be callused.

Yeah, I hear the guy in the back shouting, "My teacher doesn't train with a striking post and he's able to hit really hard! He demonstrated his power by striking one of my classmates with a punch and it sent him flying back several yards!"

Peachy. But bear in mind that if the classmate went sailing backwards, that's an indication that he was pushed! Trust me; if he was hit with a powerfully shocking blow, he'd fall almost straight down.

Like the teacher's technique, the "one-inch punch" used to be a popular demonstration technique. It goes like this: The puncher starts with his fist about an inch or so away from the receiver, who holds a firm pad against his chest. The puncher suddenly slams his fist into the pad and causes the receiver to sail backwards a considerable distance. Impressive? Nah. That's a "one-inch *push*," not a punch.

The Psychological Effect

Most people, including martial arts enthusiasts, have a fear of hurting themselves if and when they strike an opponent with full force. The result is that they often hold back when they smack an adversary. In combat, that's bad *juju*.

Martial artists who regularly train on the striking post have very little fear, if any, of striking an enemy full-force because their bodily weapons have been properly tempered and the likelihood of injuring them is minimal. Moreover, they've learned to focus the power of their blows very precisely—a skill that is almost impossible to develop without the aid of a striking post or some comparable apparatus.

Go to Chapter 21 to learn how to set up and use a proper striking post.

Chapter 19

That Extra Something

Moving from the Inside

The so-called *external* martial arts systems such as karate, taekwondo, and most forms of kung-fu often rely exclusively on the power of the larger, easily discernible muscles and body movements such as the rotation of the waist (which includes the hips, upper thighs, and lower back), the shifting of the hips, the use of the shoulders, and so on. However, the *internal* martial arts of taijiquan, xingyiquan, baguazhang, liuhebafa, and yiliquan also employ smaller, unseen tissues that are located deep within the body. This accounts for some of the seemingly strange and subtle body shifts that occur whenever certain postures or techniques are executed.

The student of an internal system must spend considerable time mastering the movements of the larger muscles and body parts before attempting to discern the subtleties of manipulating these smaller, less conspicuous tissues. This process requires a great deal of practice under the watchful eye of a qualified instructor.

How It Works

The manipulation of small internal tissues contributes to the effectiveness of technique in several different ways.

- The inclusion of these tissues in the execution of a given movement increases the amount of mass involved in that movement, thereby making it that much more powerful. This small increase in mass may not seem like much, but it actually contributes significantly to the amount of power that can be generated.

- Some of these smaller tissues provide additional support for the larger muscles, making their movements that much stronger.
- The sequencing of muscle contraction in certain movements produces a wave-like effect, resulting in a whipping action that is capable of generating considerable power due to an increase in the acceleration of the movement as well as an increase in the mass. The boost in acceleration may be so subtle that it is scarcely noticeable to an observer, but it is readily perceptible to the poor geek on the receiving end of it.

It should be noted that weightlifting is of no use in enabling you to utilize these internal tissues. However, special stretching and breathing exercises are often employed to condition them.

Chapter 20

Principles of Blocking

The *Why* of Blocking

We've spent a lot of time and paper discussing the principles of striking, but what about blocking? Isn't that important, too?

You bet it is. But first, let's address an important question. *Why* use a block? What is it for?

"That's a stupid question," you reply. "Blocks are used to keep the bad guy from using his time-travel skills and knocking me into next week."

If you really believe that, I'll bet you go home from every sparring session with some prize-winning bruises on your arms and you doubtless get smacked in the face anyway. Believe me, in a real skirmish you'll get a lot more scuffed up than that!

Blocking techniques are not simply used to prevent the opponent from landing an effective blow. Remember that in a real fight your objective is to end the conflict as quickly as possible. You can't do that if you just stand there and let your assailant continue pummeling you while you do your best to block every one of his attacks. Sooner or later, he'll get through your defensive techniques. (If Murphy-san is in the vicinity, it will definitely be sooner.)

In the traditional martial arts, blocks are deliberate, controlled techniques that are executed for a particular reason. They can be used:

- To strike the enemy's attacking limb and injure it so that he is unable to use it again. Blocks are often directed at specific areas of the offending appendage and may cause injuries and pain so severe that the fight is brought to a sudden conclusion.

- To establish a physical "bridge" between yourself and the enemy, so that you can either detect his intentions and respond appropriately or gain control of his attacking limb and, subsequently, the movement of his entire body.

- To place the opponent in an untenable position so that you are better able to apply follow-up techniques.

The Key to Effective Blocking

The key to effective blocking lies primarily in your ability to understand the concepts of positioning and distance, and your ability to use them effectively.

Positioning

There are only two basic types of positioning:

> A *position directly in front of the opponent and his attack*
>
> A *position wherein you have moved out of the line of attack*

Obviously, the safest position is the one that places you out of the line of attack. Once you have circumvented the enemy's offense you're in a good position to initiate your own counter-attack. However, it isn't always possible to evade the enemy's onslaught. It may be that you must face the opponent's attack directly.

Distance

At any given time you will be at one of three possible distances: close, optimum, or distant. Let's examine each one in detail.

Close Distance: Close range is illustrated in Figure 20-1. At this distance you're close enough to count the fillings in your opponent's teeth. Blocking techniques, per se, aren't applicable at this range because the enemy is too close. At this range grappling may be more practical. The real question is, how did you get that close to your opponent in the first place? Regardless of who closed the distance, you should have clobbered him before he got so cozy with you.

Optimum Distance: At optimum distance you can most easily strike your opponent or block his attack (Figure 20-2). However, you have to bear in mind that if are able to easily reach out and touch your assailant, he's equally able to do the same thing to you. It's a question of who gets whom first.

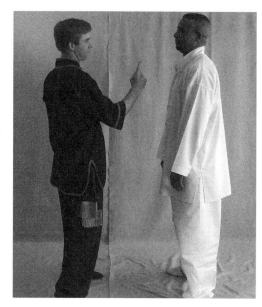

Figure 20-1

This is the ideal distance for effective blocking because you can easily strike your opponent immediately after, or during, the execution of your blocking technique (Figure 20-3).

Figure 20-2

Figure 20-3

Long Distance: At this distance you're out of your opponent's reach and he is also out of yours (Figure 20-4). In order to strike you, he will have to make a large, committed movement. Such an obvious movement is easily seen and you will have adequate time to respond appropriately.

Don't stretch your technique and attempt to block techniques that are actually too far away to harm you. Doing so can compromise your balance and cause you to inadvertently expose certain vital areas (Figures 20-5 and 20-6).

Figure 20-4

Figure 20-5

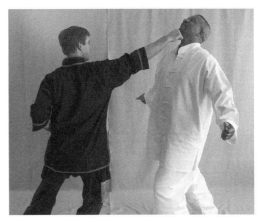

Figure 20-6

Types of Blocking Techniques

Blocking techniques come in two basic flavors: direct and indirect. It's important to understand the principles of each type. Let's take a look at them.

Direct Blocking

Direct blocking techniques are meant to strike directly against the opponent's attacking limb or weapon. They are not intended to bring the enemy's attack to a halt. Why? Because:

> *When a given movement is executed with maximum power, a second movement cannot be performed with maximum power until the first one comes to a stop.*

Don't think so? Try this experiment: Perform a strong punch (or kick) with maximum power as if you're really trying to knock someone down. C'mon, don't hold back! Really fire it out there, but before it comes to a stop, fire a second technique and give it all the power you've got (Figures 20-7 and 20-8).

Figure 20-7

Figure 20-8

What happened? Your second technique landed with all the might of a wet feather, didn't it? The power of your initial technique probably fizzled out, too. So, there.

If you're using your blocking techniques to simply shield yourself against the opponent's offensive blows, all you're doing is stopping

Figure 20-9   **Figure 20-10**   **Figure 20-11**

Figure 20-12   **Figure 20-13**

his techniques with your arms. And what does that do? It shortens his reaction time! Because you've stopped his first technique, he is able to launch a second one faster than if you'd simply ducked out of the way.

Like punching and striking techniques, direct blocking techniques utilize specific body actions and reverse breathing to give them power. You should perform them with the same celerity you would use in a striking technique. Figures 20-9 to 20-13 illustrate methods of applying direct blocking techniques to strike the opponent's attacking limb.

If you want to place your adversary in a disadvantageous position, you must first ensure that you're blocking correctly. Take a look at Figures 20-14 to 20-16. They demonstrate how initial contact is made with the techniques of the high block, low block, and inside block. Note how contact is always made with the top of the forearm rather than the ulnar or radial side.

You say that it looks pretty funky? Well, there's a reason for doing it this way. Have your partner extend one arm as if executing a punch. Place the top of your forearm against his lower forearm as shown. With a sudden snap, quickly rotate your

Figure 20-14

Figure 20-15

Figure 20-16

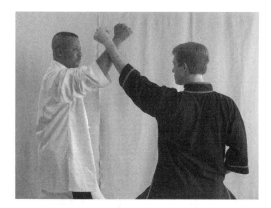

Figure 20-17

Figure 20-18

Figure 20-19

Figure 20-20

Figure 20-21

Figure 20-22

arm into the high block position. Your partner's arm will be propelled upward, exposing his entire torso (Figures 20-17 and 20-18).

This same thing can be demonstrated with the low block and inside block (Figures 20-19 to 20-22).

Indirect Blocking

Indirect blocking techniques are used to deflect the opponent's attack. You make no attempt to strike the enemy's arm or leg; you simply guide it away from its intended destination. By parrying the attack, you are able to attach yourself to it, if even for a moment. But during that moment you can detect what your adversary intends to do next and take the appropriate measures.

Have your partner extend one arm as if executing a punch. Place one palm on the inside or outside of his forearm as if sweeping his punch to one side. If he attempts to execute a punch with his other hand, you'll feel it immediately and you can respond appropriately. Even if he should try to perform a kick, you will perceive it before it happens (Figures 20-23 to 20-25).

In the Taijiquan Classics we're told that we must learn to deflect a force of

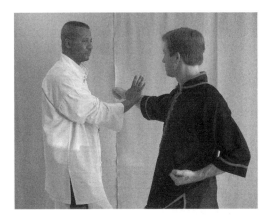

Figure 20-23

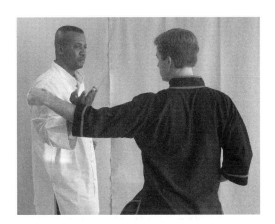

Figure 20-24

Figure 20-25

Figure 20-26

Figure 20-27

Figure 20-28

1,000 pounds with only 4 ounces. Clearly, this advice is referring to the implementation of indirect blocking techniques. No heavy, muscular force is needed to effectively apply indirect blocks. This is one of the saving graces of these defensive techniques: Although the aggressor may be larger and stronger than you, his attack can be easily diverted.

Nevertheless, in order to competently implement indirect blocking techniques, it is necessary to move out of the line of attack by simultaneously employing evasive footwork and/or body shifting. This not only allows you to form a physical bridge between yourself and the opponent; it also places you in an advantageous position from which you can launch an instant counter-attack (Figures 20-26 to 20-28).

Chapter 21

Training Exercises and Equipment

Knowing Why and How

You tightwads out there will be pleased to know that virtually all of the old-fashioned training devices that were used by our martial arts ancestors are quite inexpensive as well as easy to make. Most of our forefathers didn't have a lot of money to blow on elaborate contraptions and, in any case, fancy equipment hadn't been invented yet. Moreover, *fancy* and *expensive* don't necessarily equate with *better*. In most cases, the simplest and least expensive devices have almost always been the most effective. They still are. But you have to use them properly if you expect to reap the rewards.

The Striking Post

There are many types of striking posts, but the best I've seen is one that is planed down on one side, the side toward you. This kind of post is very popular with the practitioners of Okinawan and Japanese forms of karate. The reason I prefer this kind of striking post is because it is somewhat flexible. That is, it "gives" slightly when you strike it. The springiness of the striking post is its most important feature because it allows you to transfer your striking force directly into the post.

You should never strike something that doesn't move. Don't affix your striking pad to a wall, a tree, or a heavy post that won't budge when you hit it. Why? Okay, I'll go over this one more time. ...

If you hit something that doesn't move; something that is more stable and better rooted than you are, what happens? You will absorb most of your own striking force! You're actually striking yourself! And if you regularly practice striking an immovable object, you will eventually damage certain tendons, ligaments, and joints. You may also incur internal injuries. If you don't understand this principle, re-read Chapter 5.

It is my contention that the striking post is absolutely indispensable for the development of striking power. I know some people will disagree, but trust me when I tell you that the warriors of times past, including those who were renowned for their prowess in internal kung-fu, practiced regularly with some kind of striking post. It's one thing to strike powerfully at the air and *have faith* that you can hit hard. It's quite another thing to bloody well *know* that you can hit hard because you can repeatedly slam your hand into a wooden striking post without any discomfort.

Building a Striking Post

Figures 21-1 and 21-2 show a proper striking post, made from a length of 4-by-4 that tapers down to a half-inch thickness at the top. The top of the post will be roughly level with your solar plexus when it's installed.

Two 16-inch stabilizers are attached to the bottom of the post. The first is attached to the front, about 2 inches from the bottom. The second stabilizer is attached to the back of the post, about 16 inches above the first one. The padding can be made from a firm piece of rubber padding (about 2 inches thick) or any other surface that will provide a cushion for your hands. The pad may be wrapped

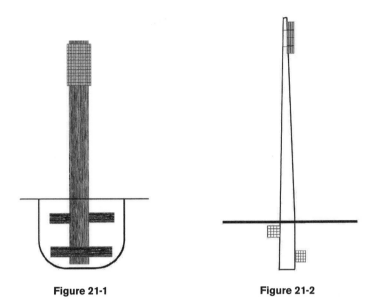

Figure 21-1   **Figure 21-2**

with an old karate belt or soft cotton or hemp rope. If you wrap the pad with rope you should thoroughly soak it in water first, then lay it out and pound it with a hammer to soften it up.

Dig a hole 3 to 4 feet deep, and about 20 inches from side to side. Pour about an inch of gravel into the bottom and set the post in it. The striking pad should be set at chest height. Fill in the hole and pack the dirt down tight. The striking surface of the post should flex about 6 inches when you push against it firmly with your fist.

Using the Striking Post

You're now ready to find out why I say that the striking post hates everyone equally. Don't haul off and hit it with your best punch! The odds are that your fist won't land squarely. It'll probably hook slightly, causing you to scrape your knuckles against the wrapped pad and thereby remove the first few layers of flesh. Don't be discouraged. It's just the post's way of introducing herself to you and making sure that you respect her and how she works.

You can strike the post with a variety of weapons: the fist, sword-hand strikes, slicing hand, back fist strikes, and even elbow strikes (Figures 21-3 to 21-6).

Begin with only twenty to twenty-five strikes with each weapon. As your bodily weapons become more accustomed to hitting the post, gradually increase the number of repetitions. If you should inadvertently tear the flesh on your hand, wash out your mouth with soap (because I know in my heart that you'll shout out a number of very colorful expletives) and apply medication to the wound immediately. Don't resume training until the injury is fully healed.

Figure 21-3

Figure 21-4

Figure 21-5

Figure 21-6

The Candle

To help develop tremendous speed and focus in techniques, there is no better piece of equipment than the candle. And like the striking post, it's inexpensive and easy to construct yourself.

Setting Up the Candle

The candle stand can be fashioned out of a dowel that is attached to a base (Figure 21-7). A disc is nailed or glued to the top of the dowel. Melt some wax onto the disc, set your candle on it, and you have one of the finest pieces of training equipment there is! The candle's flame should be at about chest height.

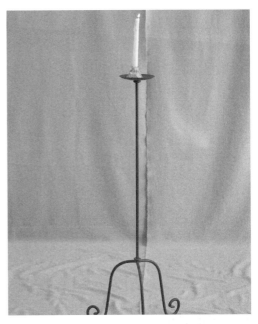

Figure 21-7

Have on hand a cheap lighter or a ton of matches. Make sure that you place the candle stand on a nonflammable surface and hang up a nonflammable backdrop because you're going to be slinging wax all over creation before you're through.

Using the Candle

The following training exercises may sound easy, but, believe me, they're genuinely tough to do and will require a great deal of practice.

If you are training hand techniques, and your jacket has long sleeves, remove it before you begin your practice session. Otherwise, the sleeves will "flap air" at the flame and extinguish it. If you are training kicking techniques, don't worry, you don't have to remove your trousers. Just be prepared to clean up a lot of wax.

Training the Punch

Stand in a forward stance and punch as quickly and as powerfully as possible at the flame, pulling the blow 2 inches from the candle (Figure 21-8). The object is to blow the flame out with the force of your thrust.

Figure 21-8

Training the Sword-Hand

Train to strike horizontally and with a circular motion (Figures 21-9 and 21-10). Again, practice to blow out the flame with the force of your strike.

Figure 21-9   **Figure 21-10**

Training the Back Fist Strike

This is performed differently than the punching and sword-hand techniques. The object is to suck the flame out when your arm whips back at the conclusion of the strike (Figure 21-11). Be sure not to allow your wrist to bend at all, lest you "flap out" the flame. Pay attention to the movement of the flame. If your back fist strike blows it

Figure 21-11

out, your technique sucks. Check to make sure that you're not snapping your wrist backward and spend some time practicing in front of a mirror to ensure that you're generating a strong whipping motion in your elbow.

Training the Front and Side Kicks

You must pull your kicks at least 2 inches from the flame. The object is to suck out the flame when your foot snaps back. Be sure that you don't point your toes when you execute the front kick, as this will "flap out" the flame. Watch the flame and make sure it is sucked out rather than blown out (Figures 21-12 and 21-13).

Figure 21-12

Figure 21-13

Training the Roundhouse Kick

As with the front and side kicks, the object of the roundhouse kick is to extinguish the flame via the suction created by your foot

as it whips back after delivery of the kick. Don't kick with the top of your instep. That'll just "wave out" the flame. And anyway, if you ever hit a bony target with the instep you'll know why it's a foolish way to kick something. Kick with the ball of your foot and suck out the flame (Figure 21-14).

Figure 21-14

Once you've developed the ability to easily extinguish the candle, use rubber bands to bind two candles together and practice extinguishing them in a single blow (no pun intended). It's quite difficult. Gradually work your way up to using three and then four candles. When you can regularly extinguish four candles, you've developed a great deal of power and speed!

The Heavy Bag

So, you think you know how to use a heavy bag properly? How far does it move when you hit it? You say it swings a long way out? Well, consider this: If it swings away from you, you're *pushing* it! I know, I know. It's fun to watch the bag swing away from you when you really crank it. It gives you a feeling of power. But the sad truth is that the swinging reaction of the bag indicates that the force of your blow has been expended on the surface of the bag rather than penetrating through it.

Focused shock won't cause the bag to swing much at all. If I hold a .357 magnum against the bag and fire the weapon, what will the bag do? It certainly won't swing away from the blast. It might "scissors." It might even jump a bit. But it won't swing back much at all.

The same thing should apply with your techniques. If your strike is properly focused so that the shock penetrates *through* the bag instead of being spread over its surface, the bag won't swing. It might "scissors" or jump, but it won't swing.

The Balloon

You believe you're pretty fast, huh? Well, here's a piece of equipment that will really test your speed as well as your determination. It's cheap, too! Simply inflate and tie off a balloon. Toss it into the air and try to break it with a punch (Figure 21-15). When you can do that, you can strike with considerable speed and shock.

Figure 21-15

Resistance Exercises

Ever see one of those ads that says, "This martial art requires absolutely no physical strength whatsoever, and it is so deadly that even karate and kung-fu masters only whisper its name..."?

Yeah. You bet.

Let me begin by saying there is no such thing as a martial art that doesn't require some measure of physical strength and stamina. However, that doesn't mean that you should immediately plunge into a vigorous weightlifting program and endeavor to become a contender for the state powerlifting title. Strength and the proper use of strength are two different things. Just because you've developed a massive chest that's flanked by hulking shoulders and burly biceps doesn't necessarily mean that you can generate any real striking power.

Resistance exercises are excellent for maintaining overall fitness. But if you're going to use them to improve your martial arts skills, you need to examine them carefully and practice those that are *technique specific*. After all, if you want to develop a stronger punch you need to practice punching! You can do squats until a certain metaphysical realm in the cosmos freezes over, but they won't help you develop a more powerful punch. In fact, such exercises tend to condition the muscles for lifting instead of toning them for punching, striking, and kicking. Our martial arts ancestors didn't have chrome-plated Olympic weights or fancy home gym machines. They used crude devices and exercises that were designed to strengthen certain types of technique.

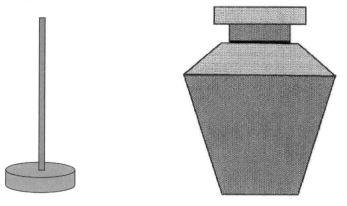

Figure 21-16. Chishi weighted stick   **Figure 21-17. Nigiri-game**

For example, Okinawan karate practitioners use the *chishi* and *nigiri-game* to strengthen their forearms, wrists, and hands for gripping (Figures 21-16 and 21-17).

Practitioners of various kung-fu styles utilize a wide variety of simple but highly effective implements. For example, the *chin-na* stick, often fashioned simply from a short length of bamboo, helps develop tremendous gripping power (Figure 21-18).

Crude wrist and ankle or foot weights were, and still are, employed to help strengthen various techniques. I strongly recommend training with similar devices.

Figure 21-18

Chapter 22

Questions and Answers

Any questions? I can't promise that I necessarily have all the answers, and some of my responses may not be what you want to hear. But let's give it a whirl anyway.

Q. **Is a front-leg kick as strong as a kick made with the rear leg?**

Absolutely not. One of the reasons for this is that the rear foot travels farther than the front foot. This allows it to accelerate over a greater distance, making its kick stronger than a kick with the leading leg. Additionally, a kick made with the rear foot brings more of the body's mass into play than a kick made with the front foot.

Q. **But isn't a kick made with the front foot faster than a kick made with the back foot?**

Not necessarily. Since a rear-foot kick accelerates over a longer distance, it's probably moving faster at the instant of impact than a kick made with the front foot. A lot of people think that a kick made with the front foot is faster than a kick executed with the back foot. In terms of velocity, they're mistaken. However, because the front foot is closer to the enemy it can strike him sooner than the rear foot.

Q. What about a jab made with the leading hand? Is it possible to kayo an opponent with a jab?

A jab isn't nearly as powerful as a reverse punch or a lunging thrust, for the same reason that a kick with the front foot isn't as strong as a kick made with the rear foot. It is possible to knock out an assailant with a jab, but developing that kind of sudden, shocking power will require lots of practice over time.

Jabs are usually directed at the head or face to disorient the enemy and set him up for more powerful blows. Using your leading hand to punch into the opponent's throat or thrusting your fingertips into his eyes is very effective.

Q. Is a jab to the body an effective technique?

In terms of getting your facial structure rearranged, yes. But by itself, a jab isn't powerful enough to inflict much damage if it's used to strike the enemy's torso. It may score a point in a tournament but it's worthless in a real scuffle.

Q. What do you think about jumping kicks?

They're nice for demonstrations and movies, and they're an excellent way to bring a fight to a sudden halt. The fight will stop because your opponent will be standing knee deep in your vital bodily fluids after slapping you out of the air like a pesky fly.

With both your feet off the ground you have no root, no stability at all. The power of your kick relies entirely on momentum. You have zero maneuverability and if the enemy suddenly counter-attacks, you are completely defenseless.

Jumping knee kicks can be effective, but I can't recommend using flying side kicks or jumping spinning wheel kicks and the like.

Q. Some kung-fu and karate forms feature hand strikes that are delivered while standing on only one leg. Are such techniques viable?

The raised leg is usually interpreted as a type of kick or foot sweep and what appears to be a hand strike is often a joint-twisting technique. In terms of physics, a hand blow that is delivered while you're standing on only one leg is much weaker than one that's delivered with both feet on the ground.

Q. In order to strike with more power, should I concentrate on increasing my mass?

You probably don't need to increase your mass unless you've been on some kind of starvation diet for the last two years and your ribs sound like wind chimes when you stand in a stiff breeze. Remember, some of the first Americans to see karate up close and personal were U.S. Marines who were stationed on "The Rock" (Okinawa). Some of them got into altercations with the small, underfed locals who, weighing in at 100 pounds or so, proceeded to pound the stuffing out of the GIs.

Trust me, you have more than enough mass. It's simply a question of learning how to utilize it in the most efficient way.

Q. So, should I work on increasing the speed of my techniques?

The more speed, the better. But just moving your hand or foot at a high velocity isn't enough. Remember, force has two components: mass and acceleration. The key is to learn to strike with maximum mass (which, as you'll recall, is only 50–60 percent of your total mass) at maximum acceleration, and to minimize the amount of power you will lose.

You need to pay attention to things like spinal alignment, dropping the shoulders and elbows, "swallowing" the chest, reverse breathing, and so on. If you ignore these principles, you'll very likely lose huge chunks of your power. If you can't remember all of them, re-read this book.

Q. **If I use the striking post to temper my hands, should I also practice kicking it to temper my feet?**

It's useful to practice kicking against resistance such as a heavy bag or a striking post to develop strong ankles, knees, and hips, and to ensure that you're making contact with the correct striking surface of your foot. Such training is also effective in teaching you how to focus your kick precisely on a particular point. However, unless you walk around bare-footed all the time, it's unnecessary to temper the striking surfaces of your feet. After all, you'll be kicking your opponent with your shoe!

Q. **Which kinds of techniques are stronger, kicks or hand blows?**

Kicks are generally stronger than upper-body techniques because they utilize more mass.

Q. **Are kicks faster than hand techniques?**

Not usually. Upper-body techniques have less inertia to overcome because they move less mass. This means that they're typically faster than lower-body techniques.

Q. **Is it really possible to kill a man with a single blow?**

Many moons ago, one of my senior students, "John," was employed at a local meat packing plant. John worked in the hog yard and one of his duties involved using an electric rod to guide the hogs into a chute that led into the plant.

One particularly large hog decided that it wasn't going to become so much ham and sausage quietly, and it attacked John, causing him to drop the rod. Hogs weigh an average of 200 to 225 pounds, and John knew that if the critter attacked again and managed to knock him to the ground, he'd be in real trouble.

When the brute charged him a second time, John stepped back and struck the animal between the eyes with a sharp reverse punch. The hog stumbled a few steps and then fell over, dead. Some time later, it was discovered that John's punch had crushed a portion of the animal's skull.

Although some people seem to be thick-headed, hogs really are! If John's single thrust dropped a large adult hog, what do you think it would do to a human? This should answer your question.

About the Author

Phillip Starr began his martial arts training in 1956 as the youngest member of a small judo club on Ft. Amador in the Panama Canal Zone. Since that time he has studied several martial disciplines which include Xingyiquan, Baguazhang, Taijiquan, a form of northern Shao-lin kung-fu, Kyokushinkai karate, and Filipino arnis.

While attending Parsons College in Fairfield, Iowa, he taught martial arts for the Physical Education Department. He opened his first full-time Chinese martial arts school in 1973 and three years later he became the first kung-fu stylist to win the title of U.S. National Champion under the auspices of the United States Karate Association.

In 1982 he developed a martial art system that he named *Yiliquan* (One Principle Boxing), which is a blend of China's three classical internal systems and a form of northern Shao-lin kung-fu.

In 1991 he was elected as National Chairman for the Chinese Martial Arts Division of the Amateur Athletic Union. Within twelve months it became the largest kung-fu organization in America and Mr. Starr was named to the Inside Kung-Fu Hall of Fame.

Starr's first book, *The Making Of A Butterfly: Traditional Chinese Martial Arts As Taught by Master W.C. Chen,* was published by Blue Snake Books in 2006. He now teaches *Yiliquan* in Omaha, Nebraska and is available for seminars. He can be contacted through the Yiliquan Association website at www.yiliquan.org.